SNOWDONIA
0 1 2 3 4 5
Miles
Conway Bay
Penmaenmawr
CONWAY
Llanfairfechan
BANGOR
nglesey
Port Dinorwic
TAL-Y-FAN
DRUM
R. Conway
Afon Dulyn
L. Dulyn
Bethesda
Llyn Eigiau
Afon Ddu
Nant Ffrancon
THE CARNEDDS
R. Seiont
CAERNARVON
Trefriw
Llyn Cowlyd
Llanrwst
Llyn Padarn
Llyn Ogwen
Ogwen Valley
Llanberis
Llyn Peris
Cwm Idwal
TRYFAN
Pont-newydd
Llanwnda
GLYDER FACH
Capel Curig
GLYDER FAWR
L. Mymbyr
Afon Llugwy
Llanberis Pass
BETTWS-Y-COED
Llyn Cwellyn
SNOWDON
Llyn Llydaw
MOEL SIABOD
Pen-y-groes
L. Dywaunedd
Tal-y-sarn
Y GARN
Llyn Gwynant
Nant Gwynant
Dolwyddelan
Lledr Valley
YR ARAN
Penmachno
CWM SILIN
Llyn Dinas
Afon Machno
MOEL HEBOG
Beddgelert
NANTMOR
CNICHT
EIDDA
PEN-Y-BEDW
Pass of Aber-Glaslyn
NANT CALL
Blaenau-Ffestiniog
Llyn Conwy
Llyn Cwm-ystradlyn
Afon Glaslyn
MOELWYN
R. Conway
Afon Dwyfawr
Afon Dwyfach
Ffestiniog
Tremadoc
N
Criccieth
Portmadoc
Penrhyn-deudraeth
Reservoir
Tremadoc Bay

With all good wishes from

L. E. Clexton

Dave Beake

H. A. C. Stallan.

J. Francis.

ESCAPE
TO THE HILLS

By the same Author:

The Magic of the Dolomites
Wanderings in Wales
The Backbone of England
Lakeland through the Lens
Snowdonia through the Lens
Scotland through the Lens
Lakeland Holiday
Snowdon Holiday
Highland Holiday
Peak Panorama
A Camera in the Cairngorms
Over Lakeland Fells
The Magic of Skye
The Surrey Hills
Lakeland Scrapbook

SNOWDON FROM THE CAPEL LAKES

ESCAPE TO THE HILLS

written and illustrated by

W. A. POUCHER

F. R. P. S.

LONDON
COUNTRY LIFE LIMITED

First published in 1943
by Country Life Limited
2-10 *Tavistock Street London WC*2
Printed in Great Britain by
Billing & Sons Limited
Guildford & Esher
Revised edition 1952

PREFACE

TRAVEL, we are told, ought to soften prejudices, and no doubt there are senses in which it does so. But I have long been prejudiced in favour of the scenery of these islands, and although I have had the good fortune to travel widely abroad, my delight in the hills, dales and lakes of Britain has grown instead of diminishing with the years. They have an elusive charm which belongs to them alone, and that charm I have tried to capture in this volume. The matchless beauty of English Lakeland, the wild grandeur of the Scottish Highlands, and the sombre magnificence of Snowdonia, all transformed by snow into scenes of Alpine splendour, make up the tale of the pages that follow. I hope my camera studies will not only convince the sceptic of the sublimity of much of our own island landscape, but will induce others to visit these places where peace and inspiration can surely be found.

For this edition, some alterations to the text and illustrations have been made—some of them because greatly increased costs of production have made it impossible to be as lavish of paper as in the days before the 1939-45 war. In some of the monographs the text has been abridged, and a few of the illustrations have been removed. The only section that has been omitted covered the Inverness-shire Glens, whose scenery is now so changed owing to the hydro-electric schemes carried out in Glens Affric and Cannich. Apart from these alterations, this volume still embraces much of English Lakeland, the Scottish Highlands as far north as Lochaber, and the principal ranges of Snowdonia.

Keen amateur photographers are always interested in technique, and the following details of the pictures in these pages may be helpful. They were taken with a modern miniature camera and are enlarged from negatives measuring only one by one-and-a-half inches. A variety of lenses was used, but the most common one had a focal length of 5 cm. (2 inches). The exposures varied between 1/20 and 1/100 of a second with a mean of 1/60, while the average aperture was 6·3 with a maximum of 4·5 and a minimum of 9. Where necessary, I employed different colour filters, the choice lying between a yellow and a pale orange.

I have often been asked to disclose the identity of the figures imparting scale to some of my pictures, and to save further speculation, I will do so here. My son John appears in Plate 25, Gerald Lacey in 129 and Ben Abrahams in 123, 124 and 125. When I took the photographs 46, 49 and 68, I had no companion, and used the delayed-action device on the camera. This allows fifteen seconds before the shutter is released, thus giving sufficient time to run into the foreground before the exposure is made.

Reform Club,
*Pall Mall, S.W.*1

W. A. POUCHER

CONTENTS

Plates are referred to in italic type

CONTENTS

THE CHARM OF THE HILLS

THE Hills of Britain are one of our greatest assets: they are a playground for both young and old, where invigorating mountain breezes and lovely views provide an escape from a workaday existence. The restful atmosphere and charming vistas of Dale, Llyn and Ben furnish that change of scene which enables the visitor to return with renewed energy and a clearer vision to face the problems of life.

This avenue to freedom does not, of course, appeal to all of us. There are those, for instance, who have a preference for the sea, or for some sport which may be enjoyed in a less romantic setting. Doubtless they find it hard to understand the love for the hills which with some of us amounts almost to a passion, and indeed to explain this strange fascination is more difficult than might at first be supposed. Such people cannot imagine the joy experienced by those who are content to while away the hours by one of our beautiful lakes, where ever-changing lights and shadows provide an unforgettable picture. They are unable to appreciate the pleasure derived from simply following some trickling burn in the barren hills and observing the feathered and furred creatures inhabiting these wild places. Certainly they can never share the delights of the mountaineer, who expends so much energy, say, in scaling peaks like Scafell Pike, Ben Nevis or Snowdon. From their summits he sees only a wilderness of hills and dales, sprinkled here and there with a gleaming tarn or burn. Yet, after resting his body from the ardours of the ascent and saturating his vision with the extensive panorama, he returns to his hotel completely satisfied with this as his reward.

It might be supposed that these widely differing tastes represent the two extremes of laziness and energy: if, on the one hand, it were the manual worker requiring rest, and on the other the brain worker needing fresh air and exercise, then the explanation would be simple. Such a line of demarcation between these opposites is, however, seldom found, and the problem remains unsolved.

Age is no limiting factor in this love for the hills, because once the affection has grown, it lasts throughout life. Elderly folk are seen everywhere at the lower levels in our mountainous country, for naturally in later life physique declines, and as a rule stamina is lacking for the ascent of the higher peaks. But these kindly people derive much pleasure from sitting by loch and tarn, and there absorbing the restful atmosphere, perhaps recalling incidents associated with the hills around them and speaking quietly of treasured memories of long ago. While in Borrowdale I used to meet one gentleman in the seventies every September. He was a retired university professor who had climbed the major peaks in the Alps as well as every well-known mountain in Britain. He was too old then to go very high, but he found great joy in exploring the surroundings of every one of the lower tarns in the district, and he knew the shortest route to them all. He was a familiar figure with his ancient ice-axe, which he always carried throughout the autumn months.

For young folk there is no more healthy vacation than a visit to the hills, and such visits have been encouraged and facilitated by the establishment of many Youth Hostels throughout Britain. For a comparatively small sum young people may enjoy a delectable holiday, moving from one hostel to another, and crossing hill and dale on the way. They may have a taste for rock climbing: if so, they can join one of several well-known clubs. There are, of course, qualifications for entrance, but the subscriptions are small and the advantages many. Sex does not make a great deal of difference to the prowess of rock climbers: the names of many ladies are held in high esteem by men of wide mountaineering experience.

Solitude is one of the chief joys of climbing. In fact, the solitary climber may ascend many of the less popular peaks and perceive no sign of life from the time he leaves his hotel until he returns in the evening. Many people think that to walk alone in the hills is to court disaster. There may be a grain of truth in this belief, but if the mountaineer is experienced—and when he is, he does not take unnecessary risks—the odds against meeting with an accident are very great. Of course, it is not necessary to fall from the face of a cliff to receive bodily injury; simpler occurrences than that have often unfortunate results. I have known cases where fractured limbs resulted from the accidental overturning of a boulder on hill tracks passed in safety by hundreds of climbers.

The thrill of height is another factor which induces many to climb. It is a grand experience to stand on the summit of any hill, even a low hill, and to scan the horizon in all directions, picking out here and there a place which recalls happy incidents and the names of friends with whom these experiences are associated. If you are alone, you look down on a kingdom which might be your own, where the clouds roll over the Glens and Bens and weave a moving pattern on the landscape. Here and there the sun glints on the waters of a loch or burn in the dim distance, and the wind seems to talk to you of the enchantment of the scene. Perhaps, far below, you espy another lone figure struggling up the crags; you follow his movements with interest, and when he joins you on the summit there are many things of mutual interest to chat about. Maybe you descend together and a new friendship is born.

The music of the hills, again, is one of their charms, for the themes change with the weather. You need not be a climber to hear them, for you may sit by a stream which prattles away on its stony bed, or sings sweet songs on the dry days as it slips quietly over the rocks on its way to the lowlands. After rain, instead of the clear notes of the flute, you hear the deep boom of the basses as the torrent plunges over boulders and rushes through narrow ravines on its way to the sea. The wind plays its part in this great orchestra when it screams through the gullies and shrieks over the ridges. Then you have to be careful, for it may easily upset your balance.

When the hills are swept by storms they assume a grim and forbidding aspect, while on the passes and in the valleys they produce effects which have to be experienced to be believed. Even by the lochs and llyns you may pass into a strange world on such occasions. The pitiless wind sweeps through the valleys and transforms the surface of the water from a gleaming mirror into a wild and turbulent sea; the foam is tossed high on the shore, while the rain pours down in a merciless stream. But if you are a true mountaineer you are oblivious of discomfort: the kaleidoscopic changes in the landscape rivet your gaze, and when the storm has passed you are perhaps thankful for having added another memorable experience to your list.

The sky is the crowning glory of every mountain landscape. You may be staying, say, at Ogwen Cottage in North Wales, and if you get up early in the morning you will go outside and stand beside the lake while the sun rises behind Tryfan. At first a misty stillness pervades the atmosphere, and then you perceive a gleam of light to the east through the heavy mist which lies in the valley. The north ridge of Tryfan shows faintly in the distance and rises to mysterious heights, its outline cutting sharply into the rosy light of dawn. Little shafts run along Llyn Ogwen and you begin to see more clearly the things around you. Slowly the mists across the lake disperse and the sun appears above the horizon, a great ball of light burnishing the hillsides with gold.

You may perhaps pass through the wilds of Glencoe when the great overhanging cliffs are steeped in mist. It swirls round their ghostly pinnacles until the deep-cut corries seem to lead up into a land of doom. The atmosphere is sinister, and you feel you must escape from this Glen of Weeping or be overwhelmed by the tottering masses above you. Then a shaft of sunlight pierces the leaden sky and a strange beauty spreads over the grim crags about you. They might now be the pillars of the nave of some titanic cathedral, and instead of wishing to escape, you want to stay and see the transformation wrought by the sun.

On another occasion you may be scaling the heights of Great Gable, the shapely peak standing at the head of Wasdale in English Lakeland. As you climb, the gentle rain ceases and your hopes run high when you see a streak of blue sky overhead. You reach the cairn after groping among the shattered rocks strewn about the summit, and although the thin mist swirls mysteriously about you, you sit down on a rock and wait patiently for that change which you feel is coming when light follows darkness. Suddenly the mists dissolve and the sun pours down on the hills stretching to the horizon, where the great cloud galleons float gracefully in a purple sky. Instead of Wastwater looking like a leaden pool below, its rippling waters now dance with glee, and the white walls of the Wastwater Hotel stand out from the sombre stretches of the dale at your feet.

On another day you are perhaps sitting quietly in one of the hotels at Ballachulish, relaxing after the walk over the great horseshoe of Ben Vare, which now frowns down upon you in the shades of evening. The sun is fast falling towards the great mass of Garbh Bheinn, which looms grimly across the wide stretches of Loch Linnhe to the west. The sky holds your gaze as one colour after another appears on its vast canvas. You try to distinguish the multitude of tints which mingle so perfectly, and as the sun sinks nearer the horizon, they assume a still more subtle hue where golds blend with greens of untold beauty. Then, as the sun disappears behind the distant hills, the colours fade into the Atlantic away to the west. A last glimmer appears on the rippling surface of the loch and then this, too, dissolves. The hills close in, your vision shortens, and night has come.

If you want to experience the real mystery of the night, choose a starlit evening and go and sit by the still waters of Llyn Llydaw, at the foot of Y Wyddfa. Silhouetted against the faint glow on the western sky is the great circle of beetling cliffs which enclose Cwm Dyli, while the waters of the lake reflect the twinkling stars above. As the moon rises beyond Moel Siabod a faint glimmer spreads across the crest of the cliffs, and you are then able to perceive more clearly some detail in the great precipices of Snowdon, while on your left the dark, forbidding slabs of Lliwedd frown down upon you. Soon, when the moon appears over the hills to the east, the stars begin to pale and the great basin of the cwm becomes steeped in a mysterious glow, with the lake spreading like a gigantic mirror right across its floor. You glance up at the towering bastions with a feeling that perhaps your intrusion on their privacy is resented, and you retreat in the direction of Pen-y-Pass conscious of having seen these sombre hills in a strange and eerie mood.

When the snow falls on the mountains a new and fairy-like world is born. You are perhaps familiar with the fresh greens of spring, when the wild flowers make a variegated carpet on the hillside and gorse casts its golden spell around, or you may know the gorgeous tints of the late autumn when the bracken has turned a deep russet brown and glows in the evening sunlight. But in the winter these scenes are transformed by glistening ice crystals and soft, powdery snow into an ethereal landscape where you may wander alone and undisturbed in a fairyland of delicate beauty. There is a strange silence everywhere; you miss the rumble of the river in the valley and the rush of the beck on the hillside. The river is now a solid mass of ice, while the beck resembles one of the recesses of an Aladdin's cave in which long, gleaming icicles look like polished spears. If the winter is severe and you happen to be in the vicinity of one of the lakes you will miss the gentle lapping of the water on the shore, but you may hear in its place the less familiar swish of steel as the skater glides gracefully and swiftly along the gleaming surface of the ice. The evergreens which decorate the sylvan slopes are heavily laden with snow, while the gaunt branches of the deciduous trees thrust up their arms into the sky, each finger carrying an adhesive band of glistening ice.

If you are staying in one of the remote valleys where a common sound is the ring of the climber's boot against the stony track leading up into the hills, you will see heavily-clad figures with rucksacks, balaclavas and ice axes, making their way steadily over the snow each morning, heading for the higher wind-swept wastes where the sombre landscape has assumed a new and gorgeous cloak. Perhaps you are staying in Patterdale and have left behind the gentler scenes of Ullswater for the bleak slopes leading up to Striding Edge, that great spur which projects from Helvellyn to the east. After struggling up the deep snow to the well-known gate on the skyline, you encounter great snowdrifts in February, and find the cliffs above Red Tarn plastered with snow. On a brilliant sunny morning these make a magnificent Alpine picture, and when you reach Striding Edge you may find the rocks heavily coated with ice. You have laughed at the supposed terrors of this fine ridge in summer, but now it is a much more formidable obstacle, and you are glad you have brought your ice axe. Here and there you use it to pass some difficult bit and then you come down to the little col where the abyss rears up to the skyline ahead of you. This is going to prove a hard ascent. There is maybe only five or six hundred feet of it, but you don't want to start an avalanche and find yourself being carried down into the depths of Red Tarn far below. So you keep well to the left, where large rocks protrude from the shaly bed beneath the snow. After a struggle you reach the plateau and make your way to the right beyond the shelter, to gaze from the summit over an immense panorama in which the massif of the Central Fells, culminating in Scafell Pike, rises into the sky away to the west. Great clouds form on these hills and you may see them drifting away in the cold wind from the north, with the sun transforming them into the likeness of some gigantic celestial palace.

Perhaps it is later in the year, it may even be early spring, and you are staying at Fort William, where the great mass of Ben Nevis calls to you from behind the town. Snow is well down into the Glen Allt a'Mhuilinn and the great ridges of the north-east corrie rise up to the summit plateau and glint brilliantly in the morning sunshine. You are going to climb this mountain and make an early start, because this expedition is one of the longest and finest in Britain and you don't want to hurry when you have reached the highest summit in the country. You make for the well-known ridge of Càrn Mòr Dearg, from which you may behold one of the grandest panoramas in the land. The going is hard across the moor, but when you reach the snowline a new exhilaration permeates your soul and you press on eagerly towards the ridge high above. On attaining it, you have a mile of undulating crest where the snow sweeps down vast slopes on either side, while you forge ahead towards the summit cairn standing just over four thousand feet above the sea. Here you halt to gaze enthralled upon the wonderful mural precipices of the corrie across the depths of the intervening glen. To the south you perceive a very narrow ridge—the famous Arête—which rises steeply to end on the summit of the Ben. You find an especial delight in contemplating its sweeping lines and plunge down the slopes towards it, ready to overcome any hidden difficulties. On your left the great unbroken slopes fall into Glen Nevis for some four thousand feet, while on your right you may pick out the Scottish Mountaineering Club Hut half that depth below. From the lowest part of this narrow ridge there is about one thousand feet of ascent to bring you on to the summit plateau, and after a hard struggle you stand there with the world at your feet. In all directions you will see a marvellous array of snow-capped peaks stretching away into the dim distance, where a noticeable feature of the landscape is the Great Glen. Its chain of lochs connects Loch Linnhe with the Moray Firth, and you may catch the light on their waters, which stretch away to Inverness. In the immediate vicinity fine immeasurable snow cornices overhang the great precipices whose walls encircle Coire na Ciste, and you may look across their abysmal depths to the shattered cliffs of Càrn Dearg, of which the Trident Buttress is a noticeable feature. If you are fortunate enough to observe this impressive scene under favourable conditions it will leave an indelible mark on your memory.

These are but a few of the delights which may be experienced in the British Hills. When young folk visit them their eyes are cast upwards to the peaks, and in their enthusiasm to climb them they are apt to ignore many of the other less obvious details in the landscape. With the coming of more mature age, they begin to appreciate such things as the wild flowers, the different types of rock composing the hills, and the birds which inhabit these regions. Imagine the illimitable field open to the botanist, the ornithologist and the geologist. The sportsman, too, and particularly the angler, will find plenty to gratify his tastes in these districts, especially in the Highlands.

The present time seems propitious for the acquisition of still more of these areas by the National Trust, so that they may be preserved in their natural state and offer greater facilities to all who wish to visit them. Several other well constituted organisations already exist for the guarding of our national heritage, and are deserving of support by every lover of the hills.

BORROWDALE FROM STY HEAD

ENGLISH LAKELAND

THE English Lake District is about thirty miles square, and covers large parts of the counties of Cumberland and Westmorland, together with a small section of Lancashire. It is easily accessible by rail to Keswick or Penrith in the north, Windermere or Kendal in the south, and from any of the coastal towns in the west. From the east, however, Shap is the only satisfactory point of entry, and this is undoubtedly the best starting point for the walker because the low hills are first encountered, and during the advance westwards the increasing eminence, more rugged outline and finer aspect of the Central Fells are better appreciated.

Good roads intersect the district, especially from north to south, and there is one fine highway through the hills over Honister Pass. Further south a rough road takes an almost parallel course over Wrynose and Hardknott Passes, but to traverse it by car, even today, is almost an adventure. Vehicles are able to reach the heads of the valleys, but careful driving is necessary to negotiate the narrow roads safely.

The comparatively small area occupied by English Lakeland results in a most compact arrangement of the hills, and this is one of its most pleasing features. Diverse types of scenery lie near together, and any fit person may walk from the sylvan slopes of one valley into the wild grandeur of another in the course of a day's outing.

In general the Lakeland landscape is characterised by a soft loveliness which can hardly fail to endear it to the hearts of all visitors. In many of the valleys trees are abundant, and vast stretches of wind-worn grass cover the lower hills. This combination, together with the lakes occupying the floors of many of them, provides a picture of exquisite charm. In spring the greens predominate, and in the vicinity of the roads and lakes wild flowers in profusion impart a freshness and attractiveness which is hardly excelled anywhere. The large areas of bracken which cloak the hillsides with brilliant green in summer turn to rich shades of russet brown in the autumn, and these colours, contrasting with the delicate blues of the lakes, provide the artist with an abundance of beautiful subjects. At higher levels the innumerable small tarns are another lovely feature of the district. They are often hidden away among the gently swelling hills, frequently crag-bound in their privacy, and in June exhibit the most wonderful display of water lilies. The angler finds rare relaxation in these places, and he may usually sit there in solitude with feathered friends as his only companions.

Judged by foreign standards the Lakeland hills are not high: few of them rise above three thousand feet. Scafell Pike is the monarch of them all, but it appears as a giant only when viewed from the south in the neighbourhood of Upper Eskdale, the reason for this being its proximity to other hills of almost equal height. Altitude is not, therefore, the magnet which draws the climber to the Lakeland hills; it is rather the proportions existing between them and the surrounding country which imparts scale to the landscape. Under favourable atmospheric conditions, when haze adds mystery to the scene, some of these peaks apparently increase in stature and seem to attain almost Alpine proportions. Many of the hills are covered with grass to their full height, with perhaps here and there a bold excrescence of crags to break the single sweep of green, and it is generally on the northern or eastern flanks that the precipitous rock formations are found. Some of these cliffs are renowned for their savage grandeur: in this respect Scafell has no peer in Britain. They are chiefly of interest to the rock climber, but in no case are they so situated as to prevent the walker from reaching the summits of the mountains by comparatively easy routes. Well-defined tracks cover the whole district, and during the holiday season fell walkers are to be found everywhere making their way to the summits. Usually these paths are safe guides for both ascent and descent in misty weather. The views from the hilltops in Lakeland are extensive, and in clear weather comprise a vast panorama from the western hills, the sea stretching away far below to end in the dim shadowy outlines of Ireland.

With the exception of one or two of the eastern valleys, all the rest radiate approximately from the Central Fells crowned by Scafell Pike, although in fact Great Gable is the real central focus of the district. The dales generally have a soft, sylvan aspect, but this changes to a rugged wildness at their heads. The principal exception to this more usual form is Wasdale, where the arrangement of the bare hills at its head, together with the grim prospect of the Screes on the south side of the lake, provide a vista of solitude and wild grandeur which at once appeals to those who prefer this type of scenery. Most of the dales are enhanced by lakes whose dimensions vary considerably, from the dainty charm of Grasmere to the stately splendour of Derwentwater. There are, however, three important valleys which are lakeless: Langdale, Dunnerdale and Eskdale, the last-named in its upper reaches exhibiting the finest grouping of hills in the whole district. The lakes themselves have usually a wonderful setting which has not only made them world-famous, but continues to attract, time and again, those lovers of the district who delight to tarry by their shores.

While the highest of the Lakeland hills does not nearly approach the permanent snow line, the winter months see most of them cloaked in white. This imparts a fresh glamour to these familiar places, and under severe conditions the snow lies so heavily that many of the higher passes cannot be used. The proximity of the whole group to the western seaboard means, however, that the snow never stays for long periods, and the sudden appearance of a warm south-westerly wind will completely alter their aspect in a single night.

The Lake District has a quite unjustified reputation for bad weather. This has come about because most people take their holidays during July and August, which are usually the wettest months of the year. At that time soft rain of characteristic adhesive qualities quickly permeates the clothing of those who are not suitably clad, and even on fine days a provoking haze clings to the valleys and lower hills. If, however, the visitor sallies forth during April, May or June, and frequently in September or October, he will generally be rewarded by scenes of matchless beauty, in which visibility extends to incredible distances, and clouds, floating in a purple sky, complete a picture of infinite loveliness.

To see the many attractive places in Lakeland requires much time and a good deal of energy, for while it is true that certain excellent prospects may be observed from the roads, the most beautiful can be seen only by searching for them on foot. To obtain the most comprehensive idea of the varied character of the scenery it is preferable to walk westwards from Shap over hill and dale, carrying a change of clothing in a rucksack and sleeping at one or other of the many hospitable inns or farms on the way.

Although the holidays of a lifetime would not be too long in which to become familiar with the whole district, it may be traversed from east to west in a week, and that is the plan followed in the few pages devoted to Lakeland in this book. The photographs portray only a few of the many moods of the district, for no single place looks the same on two consecutive days, or even at different times on the same day. The sky and angle of lighting are often the deciding factors between a superb and an otherwise commonplace scene.

GREAT END FROM SEATHWAITE

ULLSWATER AND HELVELLYN

ULLSWATER lies in a fold of the hills between the High Street and Helvellyn ranges. It is unique among the English Lakes in that it consists of three distinct stretches, each of which displays a different type of scenery. A fine highway skirts the entire length of its western shore, with access from Penrith in the north and from Ambleside and Windermere in the south by way of the Kirkstone Pass.

While many a lovely vista may be enjoyed from the road, as also from the Howtown path on the eastern shore, the best way to see Ullswater is undoubtedly to sail up the lake from Pooley Bridge. With favourable weather such a trip reveals this beautiful sheet of water at its best. The first section as far as Howtown is pastoral in character, with farmlands coming down to either shore; then the bend to the west opens up a more interesting vista, with low hills on both sides and the Helvellyn range in the background. This is the longest section, and at Birk Fell it bends again to the south and the steamer enters the head of the lake where sylvan slopes fall to the water's edge on all sides and the hills close in more steeply. St. Sunday's Crag rises majestically in the background, while on either side of it there are glimpses of both Patterdale and Grisedale.

I have spent many happy days wandering among the trees which add so much charm to Ullswater, and while it is more relaxing to sit about near the shore in the lovely ground acquired by the National Trust, there are many repaying views to be had higher up the hillsides at the back. Stybarrow Crag affords pleasant vistas of the head of the lake, but unhappily the prospect is restricted owing to the number of trees. For those who wish to see the three stretches of Ullswater there is a fine belvedere just above the treeline hereabouts, and the viewpoint is well worth attaining because the panorama is magnificent. I think, however, the best view of the head of the lake is obtained from the rocky bluff on the eastern shore just beyond Bleawick, and it is unfortunate that so much private ground hereabouts prevents the pedestrian from enjoying the many beautiful scenes for which this part is famous.

Patterdale is an excellent centre for the fell walker, because in addition to the charms of Ullswater, the hills in the vicinity are rich in scenes of varied beauty and there are also the quiet stretches of Brothers Water for those who wish to escape from the crowds which frequent the larger lake.

Helvellyn is one of the giants of Lakeland, and the highest summit in a long range of hills lying to the east of the highway connecting Threlkeld in the north with Grasmere in the south. Seen from the west it appears as a shapeless sprawling mass, its steep flanks bereft of trees, excepting near its base along the shore of Thirlmere. From the east, however, it presents an entirely different aspect, and indeed its adjacent satellites are almost equally rugged in appearance.

Helvellyn is most famous for its two eastern ridges, which run up to the plateau below the summit and enclose Red Tarn, the highest sheet of water in the district. Of these ridges Striding Edge is the more interesting because it is narrower than Swirrel Edge to the north, and provides the fell walker with the most fascinating route up the mountain. For those who shudder at the prospect of crossing this giddy escarpment there are other less interesting ways of approach. The ascent from Wythburn is the shortest, steepest and most wearisome, that from Thirlspot is longer and affords fine views of the lake far below, while the climb by way of Grisedale Tarn and along the summit ridge is the longest but least irksome and unfolds splendid prospects in all directions. These routes are, however, less attractive than those from either Glenridding or Patterdale, and that from the latter is by far the most exhilarating. You leave the Ullswater road near Patterdale Hall and follow the track as far as the finger post, where you turn to the right and then to the left along the flanks of Birkhouse Moor. On the skyline you will see a gate which gives access to Striding Edge, and on reaching it you will get your first glimpse of Helvellyn. Instead of following the track to Striding Edge you should bear to the left along the crest the whole way, and when you have surmounted the hump at the eastern end of the ridge you will look along its narrow undulations which end at the abyss. If there is a lot of snow keep well to the left, and you will soon be standing by the small tombstone erected in memory of Charles Gough, a tourist who perished there in 1805.

You turn to the right here, and after passing the shelter, which takes the form of a cross, you soon stand on the summit and scan the great panorama spread out at your feet in all directions.

GRISEDALE FROM THE HEAD OF ULLSWATER

THE KIRKSTONE PASS FROM BROTHERS WATER

STRIDING EDGE

GRASMERE AND RYDAL WATER

THE lakes of Grasmere and Rydal Water lie close together among the low hills to the north of Ambleside. The main road between this town and Keswick skirts the eastern shores of both of them, but the motorist obtains only a glimpse of their soft beauty. On all other sides of Grasmere private grounds encircle the lake, although on the west a boat landing enables the visitor to scan the immediate surroundings more closely, while he may catch an occasional glimpse of it from the road rising to Red Bank and Hunting Stile. Perhaps the most pleasing aspects are obtained from Loughrigg Terrace, a path affording delightful uninterrupted vistas over this sheet of water towards Dunmail Raise, where the hills on either side of the pass make a fine background to the scene. The island of Grasmere is a picturesque feature of the lake, and boats may be hired by those who wish to visit it.

Loughrigg Terrace falls in a long sweep towards Rydal Water, and the path skirts the shore of this reedy lake as far as Pelter Bridge, where the main road may be gained. It is, however, very pleasant to continue by the banks of the Rothay, cross the bridge and go on to the head of Windermere at Waterhead. Strong walkers might follow the road by this lovely lake and ascend Orrest Head, which is a magnificent belvedere, not only for the full-length view of this sheet of water, but also for the splendid prospect of the Langdales backed by the central fells to the west. I know of no more enchanting walk in this part of Lakeland than to wander along the path from Red Bank to Rydal, sitting about here and there in the morning sunshine and quietly absorbing the gentle loveliness of the scene.

Grasmere village is known to everyone for its lovely setting no less than for its association with Wordsworth, and many are the legions of visitors who have been to see the poet's grave in the churchyard nearby. Every lover of nature must admire Grasmere in spite of the tremendous tourist traffic attracted to it in the season. I think it looks its best in early June, when the flowers surrounding the houses provide a galaxy of colour and the myriads of rhododendrons make the whole neighbourhood one beautiful garden. The most striking part is along the road towards Red Bank. Here the steep wooded slopes on the right are festooned with these flowers, and the private residences in the vicinity must be the envy of all who pass that way.

There are many attractive walks for both old and young near the village. You have only to go a short distance in the direction of Easedale Tarn to escape into a wilderness of delight where fine trees, wild flowers, rough crags, waterfalls and tuneful becks please both eye and ear. You may sit and chat with others who love this corner of England, for they, like you, find in these beautiful places that indefinable charm which will always attract the visitor. Most folk walk up to Easedale Tarn, and quite a few of the young ones proceed into the fastnesses of the hills where Codale Tarn hides its shy face among the rugged stony places at a higher altitude. This is a grand tramp, but I prefer to scale the hills hereabouts by way of Far Easedale, where more solitude may be found and where the prospect is wilder. If you venture this way you will be rewarded by many a lovely scene, and it is moreover a splendid route to follow if you are bound for Borrowdale. The track rises to the well-known guidepost at Greenup and then goes down by the Lining Crag into the long sweeping valley leading to Stonethwaite, but it will repay anyone to keep to the high ground over Ullscarf and drop down to Rosthwaite from Dock Tarn.

Helm Crag stands like a sentinel above the entrance to Far Easedale, and it is a good walk up to the summit, which commands fine views. For the moderately energetic, however, the walk over Silver How is full of interest and excellent prospects, especially the surprise when you first see the Langdale Valley stretching away into the hills over a thousand feet below. This way will take you to Stickle Tarn for the Pikes, but it is a long tramp unless you return by bus. On the east side there are many pleasant hills to climb, such as Heron Pike and Nab Scar by way of Alcock Tarn, a small sheet of water favoured by skaters in the winter.

The longest day on the hills in the vicinity is the ascent of Helvellyn, but Fairfield more than repays one for the energy required to scale this fine hill. You leave the road near the Swan Hotel and follow the path by Greenhead Gill, where the steep slopes of Rydal Fell rise into the sky ahead. You keep to the stream for a short distance and then climb the hill on your left which leads to Great Rigg. Once you have attained the crest of the broad ridge the views are magnificent, and cover a vast semicircle from north to south, with green stretches of the Grasmere valley far below and the lake reflecting the glory of the sky overhead. It is still a good pull to the summit of Fairfield, which affords an extensive panorama in which Helvellyn and Striding Edge are a conspicuous feature of the landscape. You may descend by a stone wall to Grisedale Tarn and walk back to Grasmere by the much-used track from Patterdale.

RYDAL WATER

GRASMERE

LANGDALE

THE valley of Great Langdale is a favourite venue for both rock climber and fell walker, because there are so many attractive features within a comparatively short distance of its head. It is usually approached from Ambleside, although it may be reached over the passes or through Little Langdale from numerous surrounding centres. The first glimpse of the Pikes is obtained near Elterwater, to the west of Skelwith Bridge, when the two Stickles which crown this shapely mountain appear on the western horizon.

Elterwater is a small and charming sheet of water, daintily wooded here and there and fringed with swaying reeds. A path meanders along its northern shore, and for the walker this route is infinitely preferable to the road as a means of access to Great Langdale. Chapel Stile is encountered soon after passing Elterwater village, where it is joined by the narrow road coming over Red Bank: walkers using the path over Hunting Stile strike it higher up the hill. There is a grand prospect of the Pikes immediately after passing this hamlet, for here their entire profile is seen for the first time, together with a sight of Bow Fell above the intervening slopes of Lingmoor on the left. The track from Grasmere over Silver How drops down to the highway before the bifurcation of the old and new roads, and from hereabouts there is a good view of the Crinkles, which block the end of this fine valley. The road sweeps round past Mill Gill and ends at the Old Dungeon Ghyll Hotel, although a narrow and rough cart track ascends the steep hill by Wall End and passes near Blea Tarn before descending into Little Langdale. The valley turns to the north-west into Mickleden and ends at the foot of Rossett Gill, but the pedestrian may ascend either this steep and stony pass over to Esk Hause for the Central Fells, or the Stake Pass as a means of access to Langstrath for Borrowdale.

The Langdale Pikes are a delightful playground for the climber and fell walker, and I have spent many happy times here under all sorts and conditions of weather. This whole group of hills has such a stately appearance and looks magnificent under snow. Seen from the higher reaches of the valley, Pike o' Stickle has very shapely lines which descend in one long sweep into Mickleden. A little to the right Loft Crag is supported by the fine rock buttress of Gimmer, which has attracted many noted rock climbers and may be reached direct from the hotel by way of Middle Fell Buttress. Harrison Stickle is the higher of the two Pikes, and is remarkable for its horizontal summit ridge crowned by two cairns, one at either end. Stickle Tarn may be easily attained by the well-marked track ascending beside Mill Gill, and its dark waters repose at the foot of Pavey Ark, another resort of the climber. This extensive rock face is split by a number of rather wet gullies and is notable for a diagonal ledge known as Jack's Rake which crosses the crags from right to left.

Bow Fell and Crinkle Crags are a range of hills forming the western boundary of Great Langdale, and extend from Wrynose below Cold Pike in the south, to Esk Pike above Esk Hause in the north. They present a bold rugged appearance by morning light, which reveals the wild confines of the gill characterising the central section of the group above Oxendale. By evening light they afford a grim silhouette against the sky, often of vivid hue when the sun sinks into the Atlantic away to the west.

The Crinkles are separated from Bow Fell by a slight depression in which the Three Tarns, set amid a wilderness of boulders, are a well-known feature. To the north Bow Fell rises to a shapely pyramid whose tapering lines are best seen from Eskdale. The steep southern face of this mountain is riven by numerous gullies known as Bow Fell Links, but they are of little interest to the climber, who prefers the less shattered crags of Bow Fell Buttress facing Langdale. This is well seen from the Flats, an extensive stretch of sloping slabs falling to the north and easily explored by making a slight detour from the usual track which rises to Bow Fell from the vicinity of Three Tarns. The Crinkles are famous for the three rifts in their eastern face, Browney Gill on the left, Crinkle Gill in the centre, and Hell Gill on the right, the latter emerging on the skyline near the top of the Band. This is the long shoulder running up from Stool End to Bow Fell, and is the easiest, though least interesting, means of approach.

Blea Tarn reposes in a tree-girt setting below Blake Rigg, the eastern escarpment of Pike o' Blisco. It lies to the west of the narrow sinuous cart track connecting Great and Little Langdale and passes 'Solitary', an isolated farm mentioned by Wordsworth in his *Excursion*, Book II. This valley is enclosed on the south by Lingmoor, which also separates the two Langdale Valleys. It is an eminence known only to the connoisseur, and there is no better place in the vicinity where solitude may be found and where a summer day may be spent browsing in the heather which covers the whole summit plateau.

THE LANGDALE PIKES FROM ELTERWATER

HARRISON STICKLE FROM PIKE O' STICKLE

LOFT CRAG, GIMMER AND BLEA TARN, FROM PIKE O' STICKLE

C

THE LANGDALE PIKES FROM BLEA TARN

BOW FELL AND THREE TARNS FROM SHELTER CRAGS

ESKDALE

ESKDALE is one of the remote valleys in western Lakeland. It stretches eastwards from Eskdale Green to Hardknott where it turns to the north and ends below Esk Hause. The first section, overlooked by Muncaster Fell, is a broad green valley dotted with farms. Beyond the Woolpack Inn it narrows, and is then dominated by Harter Fell, a craggy hill frowning down upon the foot of Hardknott Pass, which carries the rough and narrow road with its hairpin bends over to Cockley Beck in Dunnerdale. The remains of Hardknott Castle stand on the low brow of the hill which looks down on Brotherilkeld, the last farm in Eskdale, where a track leaves the road for the wild fells ahead.

Those who thread the confines of this green valley from the west see Harter Fell looming ahead over the trees, and if they are new to the district, may imagine it stands at the head of the valley. When they approach Wha House at the foot of this eminence they will, however, discover its comparative unimportance, for Eskdale then bends round to the north and discloses the grand hills at the real head of the valley. The dale now loses its sylvan aspect, and the barren rocky hills close in upon the walker as far as the old packhorse bridge, which spans Lingcove Beck at its junction with the River Esk. Here this stream is famed for the many craggirt pools in which the walker may refresh himself during the warmer months. A well-marked track ascends above Esk Falls to emerge into one of the wildest valleys in the district. The gigantic amphitheatre is engirdled by many of the Lakeland giants. On the west the long scree slopes of Scafell descend to the river, where Cam Spout Crag, with its deeply shattered face, towers overhead. To the north the Eskdale Cairn of Scafell Pike rises into the sky as a shapely peak some 2,000 feet above the river bed, while on the right Ill Crag provides a striking spectacle with its curved ridge ending in a thimble-like eminence. Esk Hause looms on the horizon where the stream has its source, and the eye skims over Esk Pike on the right and then Bow Fell to rest finally on Long Top, an escarpment projecting from the western flanks of the Crinkles.

The scene is one of wild grandeur which always appeals to me, although some might think it a sombre and forbidding wilderness. I have walked here many times alone, and on one winter occasion with my son, when the snow-clad hills presented a picture of Alpine splendour. Upper Eskdale is known to comparatively few Lakeland visitors, probably owing to its inaccessibility, but I can recommend its exploration to all those who wish to find solitude among the hills and to experience that feeling of personal insignificance which is discovered only in the very shadow of the great peaks.

Eskdale boasts two waterfalls which are worthy of close inspection. Dalegarth Force is enclosed by the tree-festooned crags of Stanley Gill, and although it is only of moderate height, the walk up to it by the noisy beck is a charming excursion and one that may be undertaken by people of all ages. Birker Force is, however, less accessible, although it is easily seen from across the valley near the Woolpack Inn. Eel Tarn is another attraction within easy reach of this hotel, and in June its myriads of water lilies make a picture of exquisite beauty in a wild and sombre setting.

Harter Fell is worth scaling because the ascent is easy and interesting all the way. As you gain height the Central Fells increase in stature, and provide a panorama well placed for a display of those mystic lights and shadows that are one of the greatest charms of the mountain scene. From the high ground above Coup Park the vista along Eskdale, with Bow Fell towering above its further reaches, provides one of the most lovely pictures in these parts. There are three small pinnacles crowning the summit of Harter Fell, but they cannot be conquered without the use of the hands, and thus afford some amusing scrambling. The view is magnificent, and while the northern prospect is undoubtedly the finest, there are pleasant vistas down Dunnerdale towards the yellow sands of the Duddon.

Dunnerdale may be reached by the rather indistinct path which skirts the western flank of Harter Fell. You cross an extensive moor which is boggy in places, and on arriving at the farm of Grassguards look down upon the sylvan slopes and patterned fields of this secluded valley. The Duddon flows noisily by Fiddle Steps, where you will cross warily if the stream is in spate. The most attractive section is lower down the river in the vicinity of Seathwaite, where a track leads from the church to Wordsworth's Stepping Stones, set amid a forest of trees and frowned upon by High Wallowbarrow, the craggy eminence standing at the foot of the gorge. In the spring the banks of the Duddon are embellished by wild daffodils, while in the autumn the whole scene is resplendent with heather whose purple hue adds an indefinable beauty to this landscape.

BOW FELL FROM HARTER FELL

WASDALE

WASDALE is the most frequented and by far the best known of the western valleys of Lakeland. It extends eastwards from the broad open spaces about Nether Wasdale and ends at Sty Head beneath the beetling crags of Great End on the south and of Great Gable on the north. The dale is visited by legions of fell walkers who enter it by one or other of the well-known passes. Sty Head gives access from Borrowdale, Black Sail from Ennerdale and Buttermere, while the open fell about Burnmoor Tarn is an easy means of approach from Eskdale. There is a narrow twisting road which enables vehicular traffic to proceed as far as the Wastwater Hotel; this leaves the encircling main road at Gosforth, although those coming from the south may take a short cut from Eskdale Green by a highway which affords fine views of the adjacent countryside. To reach Wasdale from Keswick involves a considerable detour, and while it is only twelve miles in a direct line, four times that distance has to be traversed when making the journey by road.

The best way to see Wasdale is undoubtedly to approach it from Gosforth, when the most conspicuous features ahead are Buckbarrow on the left and Illgill Head on the right. It is the latter, however, which holds your gaze because there is a glimpse of the Screes above the intervening wooded country. As you approach Wastwater, where the Strands road comes in on the right, you face the two-mile stretch of these colossal stone shoots which always present a strange and fascinating appearance. There are many visitors who dislike the Screes, and in fact regard them merely as slag heaps. Perhaps they have not seen them under favourable conditions, for they make a marvellous picture when observed late on a summer evening. Then the sunlight illumines the millions of stones and boulders which sweep down into the lake like some vast avalanche and they glitter like highly polished metal, contrasting vividly with the deep browns and greens of the gullies to the west while the blue waters of the lake provide a base of incomparable beauty.

You have to be lucky to see this picture of the Screes, for generally low cloud rolls across the plateau above them and the gloomy atmosphere transforms this wonderful canvas into one of grim and forbidding majesty. At such times this sombre landscape seems to speak of deep mystery: it always reminds me of Chopin's Revolutionary Study for the Piano, Opus 10, No. 12, in which the difficult descending passages for the left hand convey a musical impression of these gigantic scree slopes dropping precipitously into the lake far below. The jagged indentations of the skyline above, peeping in and out of the swirling mist, seem like the chords for the right hand, in which the emotional melody struggles for recognition amid the thunderous undulations of the accompaniment.

If you look to the right above Wasdale Hall you will perceive the savage recesses of the two gullies which disappear into the mist above. These are the resort of the rock climber and they afford him every opportunity of testing his skill against the many obstacles encountered therein. From this viewpoint you may see the head of Wastwater to advantage on a summer evening, when the sunlight penetrates the confines of the dalehead. Great Gable then makes a magnificent picture between the sweeping slopes of Yewbarrow and Lingmell, and if the lake is motionless you may observe a reflected mountain scene which is unique in Lakeland. As you advance eastwards along the road you will get a fine prospect of the shapely lines of Yewbarrow towering above the firs about Nether Beck, together with a glimpse of Gable in the background. As you approach the head of the lake this stately pyramid is hidden by the scree slopes beneath the Great Door, but on entering the dalehead it completely dominates the scene.

Wasdale is well known as the Mecca of British mountaineers, and its situation within easy reach of the three major climbing grounds merits this distinction. The white walls of the Wastwater Hotel are a distinguishing landmark in the sombre recesses of the dale, and the Inn has for many years been patronised almost exclusively by climbers. It was made famous by Will Ritson, whose photograph hangs in the large dining room, but many well-known features, such as the billiard room, have now disappeared. A few farmsteads are the only other habitations in this wild spot, but in recent years Brackenclose has been erected by the Fell and Rock Climbing Club, and this provides accommodation for members and their friends.

Wasdale Church stands by the walled lane which goes up to Burnthwaite, and should be entered by all who pass by. The site is surrounded by yews and is the resting place of a few climbers who have perished on the adjacent hills.

WASTWATER SCREES AND GULLIES

WASTWATER ON A

SUMMER EVENING

THE SCAFELLS

THE Scafells are the culminating peaks of Central Lakeland, and a conspicuous feature of the landscape when seen from the majority of the hills in the district. Scafell Pike is the highest mountain in England, but it does not rise above its neighbours sufficiently to form a striking picture. It is, however, best observed from the far recesses of Upper Eskdale, when the Eskdale Cairn justifies the title of 'Monarch of the English Hills'.

Scafell Pike is climbed by thousands of people every year, and it vies for popularity with Great Gable, which rises in one sweep from the depths of Sty Head, the pass separating the two peaks. The great fascination of Scafell Pike is its height, although this exceeds the altitude of several other Lakeland mountains by only a few feet. The well-known track which rises to its summit from Esk Hause—the Piccadilly Circus of Lakeland—bears ample evidence of its innumerable enthusiasts. A pleasant variation from this route for those coming from Borrowdale is to walk over the Corridor or Guide's Route which skirts the crags of Great End, crosses Greta Ghyll and the top of Piers Ghyll and rises to the cairn from the col on the left of Lingmell. From Wasdale this same col may be attained by way of Brown Tongue, or Mickledore may be tackled direct.

I have stood on the summit of Scafell Pike several times, but I have only once been fortunate enough to see the extensive western panorama for which it is famous. On that cold September morning the atmosphere was of amazing clarity, and I could not only see the Isle of Man floating on the glittering sea at my feet, but I perceived also an aeroplane flying towards it above the intervening ocean, which faded away into the distance where the shadowy outlines of Ireland formed the horizon.

Scafell is just across the dip where Mickledore forms the high connecting link between the two mountains, but its grand northern cliffs cannot be well seen from the higher viewpoint excepting at dawn in the summer, when the low sun is sufficiently well round to the north-east to illuminate the great precipices falling almost vertically into the confines of Hollow Stones far below. On such an occasion the finest belvedere is undoubtedly the Pulpit Rock, because this rather inaccessible craggy excrescence stands out from the mountain side and looks across uninterruptedly towards the magnificent façade to the south.

The savage precipices of Scafell are well known to all British mountaineers, and afford every type of rock climbing, from the awkward step on Broad Stand to the very severe ascent of the Central Buttress. There is no easy walk to the summit of this mountain excepting from Eskdale in the south, but an enjoyable scramble may be had by way of Lord's Rake, the West Wall Traverse and then up the higher reaches of Deep Ghyll.

A remarkable ledge, known as the Rake's Progress, crosses the base of the climbs, but in wet weather the outward sloping slabs become very slippery and only experienced climbers should use it. From Mickledore this ledge first rises and then falls high above the scree slopes on the right, there being a very unpleasant exposed step requiring careful negotiation some little distance down. For those who wish to observe this marvellous rock face closely, there is a staircase near the base of Moss Ghyll, and by ascending it and bearing to the right, the Pinnacle Terrace may be gained. This is the starting point of several of the well-known ascents, and from it the wild recesses of the lower section of Steep Ghyll may be explored by those of an adventurous nature. During the scramble over the West Wall Traverse opposite many fine prospects of these savage vertical cliffs are visible, and if climbers are on any of the Pinnacle courses across Deep Ghyll, an excellent view of them will be obtained.

The crest of Scafell is a fascinating place on which to loiter on a pleasant day. Imagine you are standing at the top of Deep Ghyll, where the retaining walls of this chasm drop away sensationally into the very bowels of the northern face of the cliff. On your left Deep Ghyll Buttress rises a hundred feet above the rim of the ghyll, while on your right Scafell Pinnacle makes a conspicuous foreground to the shapely head of Gable away across Hollow Stones. Between these two mighty bastions you may look further to the left across the shoulder of Lingmell and along the whole sweep of Mosedale, where Pillar rises to the skyline from its far recesses. On the right of the Pinnacle and separated from it by Jordan Gap stands the fine bold summit of Pisgah. You may scramble on to it and gaze across Mickledore to the Scafell Pikes, where the well-marked tracks meander over the maze of boulders up to the large cairn crowning the summit.

If you wish to see the immense panorama to the south you will walk over to the cairn standing behind you on the summit of the mountain, where you will linger entranced by the wonderful scene of hill and valley.

THE SCAFELLS FROM THE HEAD OF WASTWATER

PILLAR AND MOSDALE FROM SCAFELL PINNACLE

THE SCAFELL PIKES FROM PISGAH

GREAT GABLE

SEEN from Wasdale, Great Gable is the most beautiful peak in Lakeland. Its shapely lines are a landmark even from the foot of Wastwater, but its importance is not fully apparent until the dalehead is entered. The mountain then completey dominates the scene, and its stately form compels the admiration of every visitor, no matter at what season of the year it is viewed.

It is fortunate that the finest aspect of Gable faces the south-west, because apart from the seasonal changes in its appearance, it alters almost from hour to hour. In the early morning the sunlight skims across its flanks and it rises as a sublime pyramid above the shadowed and indistinct recesses of the dale as far as Sty Head. At midday it is scarcely as impressive, since there is then little contrast in the flat lighting, but at eventide, when the late sun is well behind Yewbarrow, every feature of its face is clearly defined and the narrow *arêtes* of the Napes, high up on the mountain, shine like polished steel against the deep shadows cast into the intervening gullies.

Great Gable is a favourite with climbers as well as pedestrians. The latter may easily reach the summit by a variety of routes, of which that from Sty Head by Aaron Slack is the most enclosed and least interesting as far as Wind Gap. The Breast Track takes a direct line up the open fell to the left of this ravine, but it is not so fascinating as the Climbers' Track still further to the west, which ascends high above the path down to Wasdale. It passes Kern Knotts, where rock climbers may often be seen on the cracks in this seventy-foot exposed wall. It then crosses the flanks of the mountain with Tophet Bastion towering ahead, and after passing the lower scree of Great Hell Gate, rises to enter the dark recesses of the Needle Gully.

This is the first rift in the fine outcrop of rock known as the Napes, and if you climb the easy rock staircase on the left to the Dress Circle you will frequently see both men and women making the ascent of the Napes Needle, the most famous of all Lakeland climbs. This obelisk stands in isolation just across the gap and makes a fine subject against the shattered crags of the Scafell group on the other side of the valley. The Climbers' Traverse now crosses the face of the Napes at the base of all the climbs, and it is a pleasant and entertaining walk to follow its stony exposed undulations where the maze of broken crags fall steeply into the dale far below. You may pass below the Sphinx and climb down into the confines of Little Hell Gate, but it is well worth your while to scramble up into a position from which you can view this strangely shaped rock. It makes an impressive foreground to the magnificent vista along Wasdale, where you may pick out Burnthwaite nestling among the trees at your feet; then you perceive the white walls of the Inn beyond and your eye skims across the surface of Wastwater to rest finally upon the dim outline of the coast away to the west. If you go down into Little Hell Gate, the ascent of this slippery insecure scree is both slow and arduous, and you will not reach the summit with the same elation as if you scramble up the Sphinx Ridge. This rises above the rock and is full of interest all the way, for as you ascend it you look over the full length of the Arrow Head Ridge to the fine profile of the Eagle's Nest, and although you will be compelled to use your hands, the route is free from danger. You emerge at the top of the Napes with Westmorland Crags towering overhead and shielding the summit, but if you turn these rocks on the left, you will soon be standing by the cairn of this peerless peak and scanning the hills and dales spread out like a map before you.

The panorama on a clear day has a justified reputation for excellence, for in addition to the vista along Wastwater you look down the barren trough of Ennerdale or over the Buttermere Fells to Grasmoor. Further to the north you will see both Skiddaw and Saddleback standing well up on the horizon, with glimpses of the intervening dales, while to the south-east you will obtain a unique prospect of the Langdale Pikes beyond Esk Hause. The Scafell group make a serrated skyline to the south, where you will recognise all the well-known features.

There is another excellent approach to Gable from Honister over Brandreth and Green Gable, while those coming from Wasdale will tackle the steep and trying ascent of Gavel Neese, the spur above Burnthwaite. Climbers bound for the sunless, damp and slippery rocks of Gable Crag above the head of Ennerdale will make for Beck Head, the depression between it and Kirk Fell, and bear to the right along the base of this secluded climbing ground. The best view of Gable Crag is obtained from Moses Trod where it leaves Brandreth, or from the summit of Haystacks, but to perceive its face clearly, it is necessary to be in these places late on a summer evening when the sun is sufficiently round to the north-west to illuminate their surface.

GREAT GABLE FROM WASDALE

NAPES NEEDLE

WASTWATER FROM THE SPHINX ROCK

ENNERDALE, PILLAR, HAYSTACKS AND HIGH STILE

ENNERDALE is one of the longest and most barren valleys in Lakeland. It stretches eastwards from the low undulating country about Ennerdale Bridge to the moraine heaps at the foot of Green Gable. The head of the dale is more familiar to visitors than the foot, where the lake provides sport for the angler. The hills in the immediate vicinity are not patronised extensively by the fell walker, who, however, frequently crosses the higher reaches of the valley at the secluded Youth Hostel between Black Sail and Scarth Gap. The Angler's Inn stands on the shore of Ennerdale Water, and while it is easily reached by sinuous narrow roads from the west, it is a long tramp from any of the adjacent centres. The track over the hills from Buttermere by way of Floutern Tarn is the most direct means of access for the pedestrian, although it may be attained from Wasdale by first ascending one of the passes—Black Sail or Windy Gap at the head of Mosedale.

The Pillar Rock protrudes from the high northern flanks of Pillar Mountain, which is the central focus of Ennerdale and a conspicuous feature of the prospect to the east from the foot of the lake. While it may be attained from this point, it is more usually approached from Wasdale by way of Mosedale, Gatherstone Beck and Looking Stead. Here a stony track undulates across the high precipitous slopes above Ennerdale, and when one reaches Robinson's Cairn the eastern face of this well-known climbing ground suddenly bursts into view. The rock possesses two summits, High and Low Man, and part of the former is screened by Shamrock, where the gully and Diamond Slab are important characteristics. The track passes over a narrow shelf to the top of Shamrock and then swings round the stony basin above Walker's Gully to Pisgah, which is separated from High Man by Jordan Gap.

While the magnificence of the east face of Pillar is never disputed it does not compare with the sublime grandeur of the western façade, especially if this is seen late on a summer evening. To obtain a comprehensive view of it you descend the stone shoot from Pisgah and scramble up one of the gullies across the coombe. Here you will perceive a rock structure which for sheer precipitous beauty is probably without equal in the whole of Britain. At Easter it is festooned with climbing ropes and almost every course has its own party. From this side there is an easy way by the Old West Route to the summit of Low Man, but even this ascent is not for the inexperienced.

Haystacks and High Stile together form a ridge which separates Buttermere from the further reaches of Ennerdale. While High Stile has been known to pedestrians for many years, it is only recently that the charms of Haystacks have been discovered by the majority of Lakeland visitors. Scarth Gap is the dip between the two sections of these hills, and is commonly used by walkers going from Buttermere to Wasdale or vice versa. Even for those staying in Buttermere the traverse of High Crag, High Stile and Red Pike is a good day's outing, when the range is usually ascended by way of this pass. To cross both sections of the ridge is a long tramp, especially if the pedestrian comes from Borrowdale, but it can be conveniently accomplished by two parties with motor cars when each starts from opposite ends of the range and uses the other's vehicles for the return journey. While the full walk may be undertaken from Buttermere it can be attempted from Borrowdale only by those who carry their belongings in a rucksack from Seatoller and descend from Red Pike to sleep in Buttermere.

The best way to see Haystacks is to walk up to the Drum House from the top of Honister, when its shadowy gullies may be seen across the moor descending into Warnscale Bottom, together with the fine and often detailed profile of Pillar Mountain forming a magnificent background beyond the hidden confines of Ennerdale. On a clear summer morning it is possible to pick out many of the topographical features of the Pillar Rock which juts out from this mountain well above the plateau-like summit of Haystacks, while on the right the fine cone of High Crag stands like a sentinel at the eastern extremity of the High Stile Range.

Leaving the disused tram track on Fleetwith you follow the rim of the coombe, over Green Crag and past Black Beck Tarn below, and then ascend the track which passes the Innominate Tarn, one of the gems of Lakeland. After crossing the summit there is a rough descent to Scarth Gap, followed by a stiff pull up to High Crag, whence the going is a delight with magnificent views of Buttermere on the right, and from High Stile a superb retrospect of the Central Fells. While descending the broad ridge to Red Pike you will enjoy the view of Bleaberry Tarn below, and of the gleaming surface of Crummock in the floor of the valley. You pass the former and go down the steeps beside Sour Milk Gill which brings you to Buttermere after a grand day on some of the finest hills in Lakeland.

A HAZY DAY AT THE ANGLER'S INN, ENNERDALE

THE WEST FACE O
Note the roped climber

THE PILLAR ROCK
just below the summit

PILLAR AND HAYSTACKS FROM THE DRUM HOUSE

BIRKNESS COOMBE AND HIGH STILE FROM BUTTERMERE

HONISTER AND BUTTERMERE

HONISTER, perhaps the best known of the Lakeland passes, is the connecting link between Borrowdale and Buttermere. The highway ascends steeply in the first section above the hamlet of Seatoller, and the gradient is then easy to the summit, but on the western side the descent is steep and sinuous in the higher reaches of the valley, and the road then slopes gently down to Gatesgarth, where it soon emerges by the shore of Buttermere. The most striking part of Honister is when the magnificent crag appears on the left during the descent to the west, but this scene is better observed from the flanks of Dale Head, which may be attained by the pedestrian from the vicinity of the quarry buildings standing on the col. While Honister Crag merits the distinction usually accorded it, there are other less impressive but very charming prospects which appeal to the artistic, such as the tree-girt chattering beck flowing beside the road on the eastern aspect of the Pass and the view of the Buttermere Fells in the neighbourhood of the bridge half-way down the western side, where the sweeping slopes of the enclosing hills provide an excellent setting for this mountain range.

I shall always remember my early experiences of the Buttermere Round when the coach left Keswick for Honister by way of Borrowdale and returned to the town through the beautiful Newlands valley. I used to try to secure the seat beside the coachman because I loved his descriptions of the landscape as we trotted slowly along the old road to Rosthwaite, where he invariably disappeared into the Scawfell Hotel on a secret mission! Those who expected to ride up the pass were disappointed, because we always descended at Seatoller and helped to push the vehicle to the top. Then we walked down the steep parts on the other side, but rode into Buttermere with the feeling that we had well earned our lunch. The same procedure existed on the journey home over Buttermere Hause into Newlands, but I never pass over this route nowadays without hearing the familiar click of the horses' hooves on the highway, and if I am alone I sometimes look round half expecting to find the coach nearby.

This romantic journey is now a thing of the past, and the road has an excellent surface which facilitates rapid transport by car from one valley to the other. On a few occasions I drove a car over the old road, and it was a most adventurous journey, especially across the flat slabs of rock which then formed the surface below the forbidding precipices of Honister Crag.

For those who are familiar with this pass there is an attractive route to Buttermere from its summit by digressing to the right near the wire fence which leads to the cairn on Dale Head. A narrow ridge then runs to the west across the flanks of Hindsgarth and up to the summit of Robinson, and the descent is made to the village over Buttermere Moss. This walk affords unique views of the hills on the other side of the valley, because the pedestrian is high enough to look into the two coombes which characterise them.

Buttermere is one of the most romantic spots in Lakeland, and is set amid shapely hills where the lake reposes almost at the head of the dale. This is typical of the soft loveliness for which the district is famous, and the magical lights cast into the valley by the sun across both Haystacks and High Stile provide a picture which always appeals to both artist and photographer. Even on the grim days when low clouds roll over Scarth Gap and the hummocked peaks of Haystacks loom through the swirling mist, the head of the lake affords a scene of mystic beauty. I have sometimes lingered there for hours, watching the intermittent rays of the sun penetrate cracks in the cloud canopy, when unbelievable effects were produced on this familiar landscape. Fleetwith stands like a sentinel at the eastern end of the dale, eternally looking down on this scene of matchless beauty, and to live in this valley under the very shadow of these hills must be one of the great desires of all who know its many phases.

The walks round Buttermere appeal to people of all ages, and it is not essential to climb the surrounding hills to appreciate the charms of the district. The path skirting the lake is full of interest, with changing views at every turn, while the south-western shore of Crummock is also noted for its many wonderful scenes, not only of the dalehead itself, but also of the deep recesses in the Grasmoor range, where Whiteless Pike makes a bold and graceful foreground on the other side of this sheet of water. It is also a pleasant experience to saunter up to Scale Force, the highest waterfall in Lakeland, which is enclosed in a shadowy ravine, while for those who wish to advance further, there are the boggy folds of the hills in the vicinity of Floutern Tarn. Add to these glimpses of infinite loveliness the quiet gentle slopes about Loweswater, and you have a picture which appeals to the most fastidious of Lakeland visitors.

HONISTER LOOKING WEST TO BUTTERMERE

THE HEAD OF BUTTERMERE

A WILD DAY ON HAYSTACKS SEEN FROM THE HEAD OF BUTTERMERE

THE LANGDALE PIKES FROM ESK HAUSE

STY HEAD AND ESK HAUSE

To mention either of these well-known places to any Lakeland enthusiast is to evoke memories of Seathwaite, the wettest hamlet in the whole district; a gated stony path that meanders by the noisy waters of the beck; Stockley Bridge, well placed at the junction of Sty Head with Grain Gill; the steep acclivities of the shattered slopes to the left of Taylor Gill Force, where the fall is hidden by the wind-swept pines; the vista looking back along the patterned fields of the valley, above which Saddleback rises over the intervening hills to form the distant horizon; the cairned track which follows the eastern bank of the stream to the wooden bridge, so often swept away by winter gales; the first glimpse of Lingmell standing serenely in the background, quickly followed by the appearance of the large cairn on Scafell Pike further to the left, and then the joy of sitting by the rippling waters of Sty Head Tarn near the top of the pass, with the first section of the walk accomplished.

On a pleasant day this spot seldom breathes an atmosphere of solitude, because no sooner have the sounds of one party's nailed boots faded into silence on the stony track than another's strike the ear, for from this popular venue paths lead to every part of the Central Fells. You will doubtless remember peeping round the summit crags on the west to look down on the sombre stretches of Wasdale; perhaps after smoking a cigarette while resting near the first-aid post you turned your steps in the direction of Esk Hause. There was still the delightful anticipation of once again seeing Sprinkling Tarn nestling at the foot of the terrific precipices of Great End; the red banks of the stream where the Grain Gill track joins your own, and finally the elation of standing by the guide post on Esk Hause, when you scanned the undulating country to the south-east in which the Langdales are such a prominent feature of the wide landscape.

This is the principal cross-roads of Lakeland, and from it valleys radiate in all directions. In dense mist, when visibility is reduced to a few yards, it is difficult enough to find the guide post, let alone to locate these dales with accuracy.

STY HEAD AND BORROWDALE FROM LINGMELL

THE LANGDALE PIKES FROM GLARAMARA

GREAT END AND GLARAMARA

WHEN you leave Seatoller behind and walk along the canopied road towards Seathwaite, Great End rises majestically beyond the fells to the south, and if you are making for this gullied peak it will beckon to you almost the whole way, excepting when it is temporarily hidden as you approach Stockley Bridge. It is a pleasant walk into the wild recesses of Grain Gill, which many use as the most direct ascent to Esk Hause, and since you need not go as far as the guide post, you will probably leave the well-marked track above Sprinkling Tarn and take a short cut across the scree to strike the northern ridge of Great End well up towards the summit. This mountain is a splendid viewpoint, especially for the panorama to the north where you may look from Gable on the left, along Borrowdale to Derwentwater on the right, and see Skiddaw rising superbly on the distant horizon.

It is a grand walk to the summit of this peak, but to return the same way is unthinkable when other attractive variations provide a more interesting route home. Of these the track over Allen Crags to Glaramara is one of the finest, but if you are not familiar with the endless undulations of its long summit ridge, you will wonder when the final slope up to the cairn is going to appear ahead. To the south-east you have as your companions the two prominent peaks of the Langdales, with many glimpses of the hills and dales beyond, while from the summit of Glaramara you will look down upon the thin twisting line of the track which leads up to the Stake Pass from Langstrath. The descent over Thornythwaite Fell is interesting, because if you keep well to the right you may peer into the stony recesses of Comb Gill, a wild and solitary depression in the hills near the head of Borrowdale.

GREAT END FROM THE SEATHWAITE VALLEY

BORROWDALE

THIS lovely valley stretches from the head of Derwentwater in the north, through the Jaws of Borrowdale, and after sweeping round past Rosthwaite ends at the foot of Sty Head deep in the hills to the south. The first section is narrow, colourful, and well wooded, with craggy hills descending on the one side to the River Derwent and on the other to the road, while the further reaches reveal an open strath, carpeted with green fields of brilliant hue, where the higher hills provide an engirdling horizon of striking scale and beauty. This contrast between the craggy hills and the open strath is one of the most entrancing features of the dale, and while it is attractive at all times of the year, the late autumn paints its sweeping slopes with colours which have to be seen to be believed. At that time the woods are carpeted with fallen leaves which are burnished with gold by the soft rays of the sun, and the deep shades of the evergreens here and there provide opposing tones of rich beauty. Add to this the russets of the dead bracken, interspersed with the yellow-greens of the mosses, together with the gleaming white boles of the birches, and you have a picture of infinite loveliness. Borrowdale is, therefore, naturally regarded with great affection by all lovers of the district, not only for this delightful sylvan aspect, but also for its unique position giving access to many other centres by way of numerous passes over the surrounding hills.

The adjacent town of Keswick is well placed for the distant exploration of Borrowdale, but the peaceful atmosphere of the villages dotted about its strath makes them infinitely preferable centres for the real appreciation of its innumerable charms. Grange is the first hamlet encountered on the walk into the dale, and its romantic situation by the well-known bridge at the foot of Knitting How appeals to all visitors. Here there are walks on to the heather-clad hills to the west, where Cat Bells, Maiden Moor and Scawdell Fell afford many attractive views of the surrounding country. It is also a good centre for those who wish to wander along the sinuous course of the Derwent amid the birches for which this valley is famous. Grange stands in the narrowest part of the valley, and Castle Crag rises from its threshold as a shapely cone to block the view to the south. In winter, Gate Crag ascends to mysterious heights from the banks of the stream, its snow-clad summit imparting an Alpine character to the scene.

The road beyond this village in the vicinity of the Bowder Stone follows a winding course past many a craggy knoll, with an occasional glimpse of the river, and the driver of a car has to be careful in negotiating the numerous bends. The houses of Rosthwaite soon come into view on the open strath, when its situation is at once seen to merit the great affection bestowed upon it by thousands of visitors. I have always regarded Rosthwaite as the best centre in Borrowdale, because there are so many beautiful places within easy walking distance. For those who like to spend a pleasant day without going too high there is the charming stroll over to Watendlath, where the white-washed houses come into sight on the descent past the larches which decorate the hillside above the tarn. This hamlet was popularised by the late Sir Hugh Walpole, whose Judith Paris lived in one of the cottages, but today there is no agreement among the residents as to which of them was her home. The walk down the walled lane and through Ashness Woods completes an entertaining and not too tiring day.

For those of an energetic nature there is the climb up the Lobstone Band as an appetiser for breakfast, although this prominent ravine is much farther from the village than it appears. It is, however, a splendid approach to Dale Head for the walk over the western hills to Buttermere. While in Rosthwaite it is worth climbing the hills behind the village to search for the elusive Dock Tarn. The hotels are reputed for their excellence, and any visitor cannot do better than spend an evening in the cosy bar of the local inn at any time of the year.

From the small hillock nearby there is a fine vista into the Central Fells, and at sundown on a gloomy day they provide that mystic atmosphere which is one of their greatest attributes.

A feature noticed by all who walk towards Stonethwaite is the great sweep of Greenup Edge enclosing the eastern aspect of the valley, in which Eagle Crag dominates the middle reaches at the entrance to Langstrath. This long valley stretches away into the hills beyond Glaramara and is noted for its Olympian pools, where deep water affords excellent bathing during the hot summer months. Both these valleys give access to Langdale, and the former to Grasmere as well. The main road from Rosthwaite swings round to the west through the walled fields of the adjacent farmsteads, and finally reaches Seatoller at the foot of Honister. The head of Borrowdale may be attained by diverging to the left before arriving at this village, but the route to Sty Head has already been described in another monograph.

GLOOM IN BORROWDALE

F

DERWENTWATER AND SADDLEBACK

DERWENTWATER is the Queen of English Lakes and possibly also the most beautiful in the whole of Britain. It lies in the north of the district with the houses of Keswick descending almost to its shore, and is encircled by a road from which glimpses may be had of its surface, glistening away into the distance, where the mountains in the background make a perfect setting from every viewpoint. It is this compact arrangement of the engirdling hills, whose sylvan slopes fall on almost all sides to the very water's edge, that makes Derwentwater so charming. Moreover, it does not matter at what season of the year or at what time of the day it is seen, for its vistas are for ever enriched by the magical lights and shadows which afford a prospect of infinite beauty.

Skiddaw stands eternally on the north, its massive sprawling slopes descending to Keswick and indeed also flanking the long stretches of Bassenthwaite, which lies to the north-west of Derwentwater. The Jaws of Borrowdale enclose the lake to the south, but are overshadowed by the distant Central Fells, where Glaramara rises in this superb background to the left of Scafell Pike, the crowning peak of Lakeland. The lower hills on the east are characterised by the rocky excrescences of Walla and Falcon Crags, below which the tree-canopied slopes fall steeply to the lakeside road. On the west several shapely peaks rise above the woods fringing the shore, where Cat Bells, Causey Pike and Grisedale Pike form conspicuous features of the landscape.

While there are numerous viewpoints on the surrounding hills from which the lovely setting of Derwentwater may be seen in part, there are only two which have achieved any great reputation for comprehensiveness. The first is Castle Head, which rises in isolation near the Borrowdale road to the south of Keswick, and the accessibility of this belvedere doubtless accounts for its popularity. The second is in the vicinity of Latrigg on the southern flanks of Skiddaw, where the uninterrupted vista along the whole length of the lake not only clearly reveals the many wooded islands, but also the indented shore, together with three-quarters of the encircling hills.

Elevated prospects of wide landscapes generally appeal to the public, but unless they possess specific foreground interest, their magnificence is lost. For this reason I consider the lakeside vistas of Derwentwater to be infinitely superior to those from the above viewpoints, and the scenes unfolded in the neighbourhood of both Friar's Crag and Broomhill Point have been justly praised by all the great artists.

Saddleback stands in splendid isolation on the northern boundaries of the Lake District, and is indeed a fitting place from which to bid farewell to this lovely corner of England. The five great spurs of the mountain rise directly from the road and culminate in a summit ridge which is almost the preserve of the connoisseur, for its little known traverse, followed by the descent to Keswick, is one of the most delightful walks in the whole of Lakeland. Blencathra is the more romantic designation for this peak, which rivets the attention of all travellers approaching the district from Penrith. There is a slight dip in the summit between Hall's Fell Top in the south and Foule Crag in the north, and when this is seen from a distance it resembles a saddle, which probably accounts for its more popular name.

Saddleback presents an imposing appearance when seen from the Druids' Circle, a mile and a half from Keswick, but I do not consider this the best place from which to observe its fine topography. When clad in snow it looks magnificent from the Vale of St. John, or better still, from one of the escarpments of the hills enclosing the northern reaches of this secluded valley.

There are a few hamlets reposing in the very shadow of Blencathra, and its ascent may be begun from any of them. The more direct route to the cairn is up the narrow rocky spur leading to Hall's Fell Top, and while it is an interesting climb, better prospects are obtained by following the crest of the ridge rising from Scales. An alternative ascent is by way of Scales Tarn, deeply hidden in the eastern folds of this great mountain and frowned down upon by Sharp Edge, an *arête* which looks more difficult than it is. This affords remarkable views of the dark crag-encircled waters far below, and leads up to Foule Crag, which is half a mile to the north of the summit.

Hall's Fell Top is an admirable belvedere, and commands an extensive panorama stretching from east to west. To the south-east you look along the full length of the High Street Range, where Ill Bell appears as a white cone at its southern extremity. The Helvellyn Range is seen end-on, and as such is not impressive, but this is compensated for by the charming vista on the right which carries the eye over the Vale of St. John to rest finally upon the tree-girt waters of Thirlmere. Further to the south-west the scene is magnificent. Here you look down upon the gleaming surface of Derwentwater, above which all the familiar peaks from Gable to Grisedale Pike rise into the background.

DERWENTWATER AT EVENTIDE

CAUSEY PIKE AND GRISEDALE PI

FROM FRIAR'S CRAG ON CHRISTMAS DAY

SKIDDAW FROM THE LANDING STAGES

SADDLEBACK FROM THE DRUIDS' CIRCLE

THE SCOTTISH HIGHLANDS

THE Highlands occupy a large area of Scotland, and are situated approximately north of a line drawn between Glasgow and Aberdeen. Several well-defined groups of hills are spread throughout these northern latitudes, and both English Lakeland and Snowdonia are insignificant in size when compared with them. For instance, the Lake country covers about the same area as the Cairngorms, while Snowdonia is roughly equal to that part of the Central Highlands lying between Glencoe and Roy Bridge. Distances in Scotland are therefore great, and this fact has to be borne in mind when visiting the district. Moreover, north of Fort William accommodation is scarce, and in a normal high season the wayfarer would of necessity make sure of his sleeping quarters well in advance.

South of the Great Glen the Highlands are intersected by many excellent highways, but north of this dividing line roads are narrow and have poor surfaces, with the exception of one or two main roads running over to the west coast. Accessibility from Edinburgh and Glasgow is in consequence relatively easy by motor car, and two railway systems serve the outlying districts, the one from Glasgow to Mallaig and the other from Inverness to the Kyle of Lochalsh. Both these lines pass through magnificent country, the southern one in particular revealing grand prospects of many of the fine hills in Scotland.

One of the great attractions of the Highlands is their proximity to the sea, for the deeply indented coastline brings the lochs many miles inland. This fact has a direct bearing upon the length of any ascent, because in many cases altitude has to be calculated on the basis of a start from sea level and not from 500 or 1,000 feet as is often the case in England and Wales. Many of these hills typify wild mountain grandeur at its best, but it does not follow that this attractive aspect may always be seen from the roads. It is true that the splintered pinnacled ridge of the Coolins may be seen from afar by any observer, as also may the weird outline of the Cobbler or the shattered buttresses of Bidean nam Bian, but in many instances the grandest aspects are revealed only to those who search for them. For example, Ben Nevis appears as a gigantic grassy hump seamed with innumerable burns when seen from the borders of Loch Linnhe, whereas its north-eastern façade is one of the most magnificent in the whole country, but may be observed only by the pedestrian who is prepared either to walk into the recesses of the Glen Allt a'Mhuilinn or to climb the great ridge leading to Càrn Mòr Dearg. The ridges of the Highlands are perhaps known best to the mountaineer, and many of them are unique. It is necessary to mention only Aonach Eagach, which rises for some 3,000 feet to enclose Glencoe on the north. This long ridge is characterised by its narrowness and by the array of shattered pinnacles which totter on the very edge of vast precipices, and from whose crest the climber has little chance of escape. The corries are another remarkable feature of these hills. In many of them the rock architecture attains superb proportions, as, for instance, Toll an Lochain in the An Teallach Hills, or Coire Mhic Fhearchair on Beinn Eighe.

The Scottish glens are world-renowned for their different types of scenery. This varies from the often sinister appearance of Glencoe or the sublime solitude of Glen Sligachan to the dainty wooded aspect of the Trossachs or the incomparable enchantment of Glen Affric, where the combination of bubbling burn, chattering cascade, silent loch and birch-clad hillside provide a picture which has always appealed alike to both artist and photographer. The moors in the Highlands cover extensive areas, and among sportsmen are famed for their grouse. It is, however, possible to wander over them out of season and experience the most utter loneliness imaginable. Rannoch Moor is perhaps the most famous of them scenically: here peat hags, small lochans and boulder-strewn undulations make up the great plateau which is surrounded by some of the most shapely peaks in Scotland.

The lakes are probably the most attractive feature in this country, so abundantly rich are they in scenes of great beauty. There are both inland and sea lochs, and each have their own special charms. Of the former Loch Lomond is possibly the best known owing to its accessible position, Loch Maree the most exquisitely beautiful, with its many islands and fine surrounding hills, and Loch Coruisk in Skye the grandest, with its forbidding splintered spires and savage precipices encircling the skyline; while of the sea lochs, Loch Hourn has probably the most favoured reputation for wild grandeur. One of the great advantages of the loch scenery is that it may easily be observed from the roads which usually follow one or other of its shores. The preference for any particular lake may quite easily be influenced by the time of year when it is seen, because in the autumn the purple heather imparts such a subtle colouring to the hillsides and this, contrasting with the blues of the water, together with magnificent cloudscapes, might well transform one of the less lovely sheets of water into a scene of incomparable splendour. Conversely one of the most famed lochs, if frequently seen in gloom, might for ever create an unfavourable impression.

The weather in the Highlands is subject to great variation owing to the wide distribution of the hills. Rainfall is the highest near the western seaboard and reaches its peak in the Ben Nevis district; it is considerably lower in the southern Highlands and lower still in the east near the Cairngorms. In this respect the whole district has a poor reputation, but this is largely due to the fact that most travellers visit it during the wettest months. In a normal season the drier period is in the spring, when north-west winds bring sunny days with fine clouds. The landscape then looks its best, especially if there has been a late fall of snow and the higher hills are still cloaked in white. The summer days are long in these northern latitudes, and in consequence it is possible to stay out late on the hills. Even at midnight it is seldom really dark, and there is little possibility of being accidentally benighted. Snow conditions are more common in Scotland than in either Lakeland or Snowdonia, and with the mountaineer snow expeditions therefore take precedence over rock climbing, although of course in the later months of the year the Coolins, Ben Nevis and Glencoe, to mention only a few places, provide a rock climber's paradise. The chief attraction of these hills, however, is undoubtedly that of ridge wandering—a pleasant, safe and easy form of mountaineering.

To obtain any comprehensive idea of the Highlands in one visit is impossible: even with the use of a car it is feasible to gain only a rough idea of one section of the country in a normal holiday. In the absence of a car a bicycle offers the best opportunities of seeing the district, which may be reached in the first instance by one of the railways. Suitable tours might be worked out by reference to one of the guide books, but if the scheme adopted in these pages is followed, much of the beauty of a particular part may be seen conveniently, and on further visits exploration might be continued on the same lines. To obtain even a glimpse of the scenes portrayed herein requires about three months, providing suitable weather conditions are awaited for each walk or climb.

THE GLENCOE HILLS FROM BEN VARE

ARRAN

THE Island of Arran floats like a jewel on the Firth of Clyde, a sheet of water justly famed for its beauty. It is well seen from the coast of Ayrshire, some twelve miles away, when the strange formation of its mountains shows up in the morning light. At sundown its weird peaks provide a magnificent silhouette as they rise into the western sky, often aglow with every colour of the spectrum.

The island is kidney shaped and some twenty miles long by ten miles broad. The granite hills stand to the north of the String Road, and indeed occupy almost the whole of the northern part of the island, while the rest of it is covered by gently swelling, heather-clad moorland on which a few farmsteads afford the only relief.

Brodick is the principal town, and may be easily reached from Glasgow by rail and steamer. It is a good centre from which to explore, although other places such as Corrie, Lamlash and Whiting Bay have their own peculiar charms. The situation of Brodick is most attractive. Its houses extend along the southern shore of its beautiful sand-rimmed bay, which is crowned by the shapely cone of Goat Fell to the north. The Arran Hills appear somewhat foreshortened from this viewpoint, but from the Clauchland Hills at the back of the town their wonderful topography is more clearly visible, from Beinn Nuis in the west, over the serrated ridges of A'Chir and Cir Mhòr, to Goat Fell in the east. The coast line of Arran is remarkable for certain cliff formations such as the Fallen Rocks in the north and the King's Caves and Drumadoon Point in the west, while the white-washed cottages dotted among the gorse and rhododendrons fringing the shore afford a delightful picture.

The Hills of Arran possess a strange fascination for the mountaineer. There is nothing else quite like them in Britain, for almost every type of rock is found in their small compass. Possibly the Cyclopean Walls are their most remarkable characteristic. They are found in various parts of the hills, but probably the finest examples are the pinnacles on the Goat Fell ridges and the isolated bluff to the north of Beinn Tarsuinn, near the col giving access to A'Chir.

Two wild and desolate glens separate the Goat Fell massif from the Central Ridges, and both are accessible from either Brodick or Corrie. Glen Rosa sweeps round in a vast semicircle from Invercloy in the south and ends at the Saddle to the east of the strange obelisk of Cir Mhòr. Glen Sannox extends southwards from Sannox Bay to meet it at this point, and the walk through the two glens is a splendid day's excursion. In the spring you leave the glittering display of gorse in the vicinity of Brodick Bay and enter the narrow Glen Shant between forests of larch. When the trees have been left behind, you follow the burn with bleak hills falling steeply on either side and the shapely peak of Beinn Nuis crowning the horizon ahead. A bend in the valley first reveals the Central Ridges and A'Chir, and then as Glen Rosa opens up to the north, Cir Mhòr rises at the head of the valley. As you advance towards the Saddle the savage rift of the Carlin's Leap rivets your gaze, and then you finally stand upon the col and look down on to the barren floor of Glen Sannox far below. The better impression of this gloomy glen is obtained, however, from its open strath near the sea, where the graceful lines of Coich na h'Oighe make a striking foreground, with the shadowy serrated outlines of Cir Mhòr and Suidhe Fhearghas sweeping across the distant skyline.

To climb Goat Fell should be one of the ambitions of every mountaineer, not because the ascent is difficult—it is actually an easy two hours' walk—but because the panorama from the summit is so fascinating and diverse, with the blue sea on one side and the fantastic granite peaks on the other. Imagine you are standing by the cairn with vast precipices falling over two thousand feet into Glen Rosa and the ridges of Beinn a'Chliabhain, Beinn Tarsuinn and A'Chir receding on the western horizon. The steep cliffs of Cir Mhòr rise above the Saddle and form the central focus of these hills. To the right the shattered face of the Peak of the Castles provides a vast background, with the ridge sweeping across the skyline to be broken at the Carlin's Leap by a fearsome ravine, and then to drop slightly to the north, where Fhearghas's Seat looks down upon the wild stretches of Glen Sannox. To the south and east the blue sea shimmers in the distance where the dim shadowy outline of the indented coastline forms the limit of your vision. You will scramble along the ridge to North Goat Fell, where the pinnacles of Cyclopean structure provide amusing obstacles, and if you continue ahead over Mullach Buidhe you will finally look down upon the intersecting ledges of the Coich na h'Oighe precipices which fall into the Devil's Punch Bowl far below on the right.

A'Chir is one of the finest expeditions on the island. On its narrow granite ridge a *mauvais pas* provides a sensational point in the traverse.

THE PEAK OF THE CASTLES AND THE CARLIN'S LEAP FROM NORTH GOAT FELL

THE ARRAN HILLS FRO

BOVE BRODICK BAY

THE TROSSACHS

THE Bristly Country, as this is called, lies about eight miles to the west of Callander, and is one of the show places within easy distance of Glasgow. It is a valley extending from Brig of Turk, near Duncraggan, in the east, to the foot of Loch Katrine in the west. Innumerable birches cloak the lower slopes of the adjacent hills, and provide a charming setting for the rippling waters of Loch Achray. The whole of this glen is dominated by Ben Venue, a glossy peak rising to the south of Loch Katrine, which is well seen as the district is approached from the east.

My early recollections of the Trossachs were obtained in the course of a circular tour from Glasgow, when the roads through the glen beyond Loch Achray were crowded with cars and enlivened by dancing children whose gyrations were performed to the music of kilted pipers. There was insufficient time to search for solitude in such surroundings, and we boarded the steamer which sailed across Loch Katrine to Stronachlachar and then travelled by coach to Inversnaid on Loch Lomond by way of Glen Arklet *en route* for Glasgow.

I returned to the district under war-time conditions, when the empty roads and complete absence of crowds were more to my taste, and I was indeed able to enjoy the real charm which permeates this corner of delight. I walked into the Trossachs from Callander on a hot day in May, and scarcely saw a car or another human being until I arrived at the Trossachs Hotel. The environs of Callander are well known for their soft colourings, especially where Ben Ledi frowns down upon this delightful country from the north. The approach to Loch Vennacher is scarcely impressive, as the rolling hills are too low and lack any marked features. About half-way along this lake, Ben Venue appears ahead above the trees which herald the approach of the Trossachs. The road drops gently to Duncraggan, where pines and birches decorate the approach to Glen Finglas on the right, and then after you have passed Brig of Turk, the Trossachs proper is entered.

It was the glamour of Sir Walter Scott's writings which doubtless first induced visitors to explore it. The road, under its leafy canopy, meanders by the shore of Loch Achray, with glimpses here and there of Ben Venue towering into the sky on the left, and the island in the lake just visible below the highway. In an open space fringed with trees, and at the foot of Sron Armailte, stands the Trossachs Hotel, a modernised Scottish baronial hall. Beyond it the road disappears into the galaxy of birches, and wending its way by many a craggy knoll, ends at the pier of Loch Katrine, set amid rustic surroundings at the very foot of Ben Venue.

There are many lovely walks here, and it is a joy to sit peacefully in the shadow of the trees where the white boles of the birches contrast exquisitely with the gleaming leaves above and the yellow mosses below. Some will wander along the road which skirts the northern shore of Loch Katrine and passes Ellen's Isle, so beautifully placed in these sylvan environs. Others will walk up the easy path to the craggy hummocks on Ben Venue, or perhaps thread the moorland solitudes to the south in the direction of Aberfoyle, while a few may explore the boulder-strewn slopes rising to Bealach nam Bo.

The climber, however, will cast his eyes upwards to the rocky cone of Ben A'an, a diminutive but shapely excrescence, well seen above the trees from the vicinity of the Trossachs Hotel. This may be reached in an hour by way of a delightful path which rises across the hillside beneath the trees, and then crosses the heather-clad moorland to the base of the final slopes to the cairn. The pedestrian will ascend to the col on the right of the peak, while the mountaineer will scramble round the crags to the left in search of a more interesting route to the summit. Here large slabs of rock, set at steep angles, lead upwards with a maze of heather growing from the intervening cracks, and to scale these slippery obstacles is a joyous diversion from the usual ascent. To the south, closely planted spruces decorate the head of Loch Katrine, glittering brilliantly at the foot of Ben Venue. To the west this lovely loch shimmers away into the distance, where the giants of Arrochar provide a stately undulating horizon.

BEN VENUE AND LOCH KATRINE FROM BEN A'AN

LOCH LOMOND AND THE COBBLER

LOCH LOMOND is a favourite with every visitor to Scotland. When seen under good conditions the colouring of its surroundings doubtless raises it to one of the foremost positions among the Scottish lakes. It lies within easy reach of Glasgow, which no doubt accounts for much of its popularity, but its southern extremity near this city is much less attractive than the northern reaches about Ardlui. If these are not seen a misleading impression is gained of the loch's real charm.

It is over 22 miles long and its broad southern reaches are crowded with islands. It narrows in the vicinity of Luss, and from here to its head the shores are not only beautiful, but the vistas to the north are superb. The best way to see Loch Lomond is to sail up the lake from Balloch, when the winding course followed by the steamer enables the traveller to observe advantageously both shores, together with the hills in the background.

Most wayfarers are familiar with the splendid highway skirting the western shore of the loch, from which many lovely vistas may be obtained, especially between Luss and Ardlui. At Inverbeg the tiered slopes of Ben Lomond are seen to rise above Rowardennan across the lake, where legions of climbers have landed to set foot on the track leading to the summit of the Ben. Hereabouts the steep acclivities on both sides of the loch are well covered with trees, and in the advance northwards many charming glimpses are obtained through them of the indented shores. The most surprising and indeed the best of these comes at a point when the road sweeps round below Beinn Bhreac and the narrower middle section becomes visible. Here the waters of the lake ripple away into the distance, where Ben Vorlich provides a rugged mountainous skyline: the tree-girt sandy bays, together with the colourings of sky, hillside and loch, make a picture of infinite charm.

Two small wooded islands rest on the bosom of Loch Lomond in its higher reaches, one near Tarbet and the other opposite Inversnaid. When observed by early morning light Tarbet makes an exquisite subject, with the shadowy hills rising in the background above the glimmering waters of the lake. Inveruglas Island is quite near the western shore in the remoter stretches of the loch, and is well seen from the railway which sweeps round it in a wide semicircle high on the hillside, with excellent views of the shapely peak of Ben Lomond rising into the sky beyond.

Tarbet is splendidly situated for the exploration of this district, and possesses the additional advantage of giving easy access to the Cobbler. The weird outline of this peak fixes the gaze of all travellers as the train approaches the head of Loch Long, and from this higher viewpoint, as also from the vicinity of Arrochar, Ben Arthur provides a canvas which is unique in this part of the Highlands. In recent years the mountain has achieved great popularity with climbers who are able to reach it in a short time from Glasgow. The ascent offers no difficulties and the road is deserted at the head of Loch Long before it swings round to disappear into Glen Croe on the way to Rest and be Thankful—a pass well known to motorists going over to Inveraray. A path crosses the steep flanks of the hills and leads into the lower corrie, from which this bizarre peak is well seen.

Imagine you are standing amid the chaos and desolation of the boulder-strewn acclivities above the burn and looking towards the Cobbler. The summit ridge engirdles the vast amphitheatre of the higher corrie and the small excrescence on the left, familiarly known as the Cobbler, is the highest point on the mountain. On his left rises the pyramid of the South Peak, often referred to as the Cobbler's Wife, while the strange fantastic overhanging rocks of the North Peak on the right are known as the Cobbler's Last. You cross the burn and climb up through the maze of boulders into the higher corrie, a picture of wild desolation. From here you may attain the summit ridge by a variety of easy ways. When you have reached it you will climb carefully on to the North Peak, where the sensational lines of the vast overhang make an excellent frame for Ben Lomond rising to the east above the intervening waters of Loch Long and Loch Lomond. You may walk along the undulating crest of the mountain to the comparatively diminutive rocks of the Cobbler, where you will gaze upon a wide landscape comprising ben, glen, loch and sea, all stretching away beyond the sunrise and the sunset. You may descend a steep stony track to the South Peak, but the ascent of the Cobbler's Wife is not for you unless you are a rock climber. From here you may either walk down into the upper corrie or traverse the lower peak on the south side, following the grassy ridge enclosing the lower corrie and so join the path beyond the burn which leads back to Loch Long.

THE COBBLER

BEN LUI, LOCH AWE AND BEN CRUACHAN

BEN LUI is the crowning peak in a group of hills lying to the west of Crianlarich and enclosed on the north by the road and railway between Tyndrum and Dalmally. It is also a conspicuous feature of the landscape east of Loch Awe, but this is its least interesting aspect. A glimpse of its finest profile is obtained from the West Highland Railway about a mile to the east of Tyndrum Station, when it is seen rising at the head of the Coninish valley, its striking north-eastern corrie immediately appealing to the eye of the mountaineer.

The shortest route to the summit of Ben Lui is from the Dalmally road up the northern ridge. While it is entertaining enough, this approach has certain disadvantages. For instance, you ascend with the sun in your eyes and descend to the east when the corrie is in shadow, whereas if the route is reversed, the morning sunlight illuminates every detail of the corrie. This adds considerably to the interest of the climb, and, moreover, the descent is infinitely more attractive with the afternoon sun playing upon the grand array of peaks, including Ben Cruachan, which form the southern boundary of the Central Highlands. In this case those who do not wish to go down the northern ridge may skirt the western corrie and traverse Ben-a-Clee in the descent to Socach.

Loch Awe is a long and narrow sheet of water stretching for some 25 miles from Ford in the south to the Pass of Brander in the north. It differs from the majority of British lakes in that the grandest scenes are to be found at its foot. The low pastoral country about the head contrasts strangely with the majestic aspect of its lower reaches, where Ben Cruachan frowns down upon the lovely islands and wooded slopes.

A road winds along the eastern shores, and at Dalmally joins the Oban highway, which threads the wood-shagged declivities of Ben Cruachan to emerge finally into open country to the west of the Pass of Brander. From these roads many fascinating glimpses are obtained of this lovely lake, but the most comprehensive prospects of the mountain group are seen from the low hills between Port Sonachan and Cladich. These higher viewpoints reveal the relationship between the various tops of the range, and, moreover, indicate its immensity as well as the enormous corrie whose lip hangs above the Falls of Cruachan.

The River Orchy enters the north-eastern arm of Loch Awe where the ruin of Kilchurn Castle stands on a small peninsula. It is a striking feature of the eastern vista from the Loch Awe Hotel, where Ben Lui is the prominent mountain on the skyline. The Pass of Brander begins to the west of the Falls of Cruachan, and is reminiscent of one of the smaller Norwegian fiords. The south side is enclosed by bare precipitous crags, while the opposite shore carries both road and railway. These thread the densely wooded escarpments of Ben Cruachan, which in spring are carpeted with wild flowers, especially violets and primroses.

Ben Cruachan is the highest of eight tops in the group of hills lying to the north of Loch Awe, and its tremendous bulk covers an area of no less than 20 square miles. Its eastern corrie is a conspicuous feature in the approach from Dalmally, while the Taynuilt Peak, by reason of its fine outline, is the principal object of interest in the view from the west. The southern aspect is impressive, but the mountain is seen at its best from Bidean nam Bian in the Glencoe hills to the north.

The tourist route to the summit is by way of the Falls of Cruachan into the corrie and then up to the left to the Cuanail-Cruachan col, whence the cairn is easily reached. While this ascent is the shortest, it is the least interesting. To traverse the ridges from east to west makes a long and arduous day, but it reveals the true form of the group and should be chosen as the best means of approach by all mountaineers. You first scale the steep slopes behind the Loch Awe Hotel, which give access to the broad grassy ridge connecting Monadh Driseig with Ben Vourie. You then follow the crest past the fine rock buttresses descending into the Allt Coire Ghlais on the right, and after passing the summit, scramble down the shattered slopes to the col which leads to Stob Garbh. It is only a short distance to Stob Diamh, from which you obtain a magnificent vista along the main ridge from east to west, with the summits of Ben Cruachan and the Taynuilt Peak peeping over Drochaid Glas. The walk across the intervening bealach is interesting, with a steep drop into the corrie on the right, and it is a good scramble on to this top which reveals the great riven precipices falling towards Glen Noe on the north.

The high narrow ridge rising to the summit of Ben Cruachan is about a mile long, and is split by numerous gullies on the right, in which the snow lies until late in the spring. The cairn stands on a small rocky eminence and commands extensive views in all directions.

BEN LUI FROM CONINISH

EARLY MORNING BY LOCH AWE AND KILCHURN CASTLE

THE EASTERN RIDGE OF BEN CRUACHAN

RANNOCH MOOR AND GLENCOE

THE vast area of Rannoch Moor occupies a colossal triangle with its points on Altnafeadh, Loch Rannoch and Loch Tulla. It is a stony, undulating wilderness, interspersed with bogs and peat hags. A few small lochans, an occasional burn, and two large lochs provide the only relief in this empty solitude. The new Glencoe Road intersects the moor between Bridge of Orchy and Altnafeadh, while the now disused part of the old road threads the Bà Pass and joins it in the vicinity of Kingshouse. There is a driving road from this inn to the Black Corries Lodge which gives access to Loch Laidon and ultimately to Rannoch Station on the West Highland Railway.

Loch Bà is a remarkable feature of Rannoch Moor, and is well seen from the road, but its grim solitude is not to be compared with the delightful aspect of Loch Tulla further south. This lies at the foot of the Blackmount in a tree-girt setting, beyond which the peaks of this group form the horizon to the north-west. The shore is charming, with its sandy bays and innumerable trees, and the austerity of the northern slopes is relieved by the Blackmount Lodge set amid a forest of pines. Dominating all is Stob Ghabhar, which rises well in the background. The Inveroran Inn lies beyond Loch Tulla and the road serving it ends at Victoria Bridge, but its situation is well suited for the exploration of the Ben Starav group of hills to the west and for expeditions into the wild recesses of Clach Leathad to the north.

Kingshouse stands in an isolated position on Rannoch Moor and from its windows at the back a view is obtained of the magnificent hills encircling the western horizon. The most striking of them is undoubtedly Stob Dearg, the northern peak of Buachaille Etive Mòr, whose long ridge encloses Glen Etive on the west. It is a superb black cone of shattered rock, and rises in one sweep from the plateau to end at the cairn standing above the Crowberry Ridge and North Buttress.

To the south of Kingshouse the shapely hills forming the northern boundary of the Blackmount make a picturesque grouping, especially when seen in early spring with the winter snows still capping their summits. The most prominent of these is Sròn na Crèise, whose steep western flanks enclose Glen Etive opposite Buachaille Etive Mòr.

When the old road gave access to Glencoe the only wayfarers who were able to see this magnificent valley were those who either adventured through it in a car, or tramped with their rucksacks from Kingshouse to Clachaig. The opening of the new road, however, has revealed the wonderful rock architecture of the glen to the million. Even to those who have not visited Glencoe the name is familiar, recalling the massacre of the Macdonalds by the Campbells in 1692. Scenically the valley differs from the majority of the Highland Glens in that the grandest view of it is obtained from its head.

As you go westwards from Kingshouse, the highway enters Glencoe beyond Altnafeadh, where there is a fine prospect of the Lairig Gartain on the left and the Devil's Staircase is seen rising over the hills on the right to Kinlochleven. The valley soon closes in, and the road bends sharply to the left and disappears into the gorge. Instead of following it, the better course is to advance along the old road, for the higher viewpoint reveals to greater advantage the magnificent buttresses of Bidean nam Bian on the left. This road bends sharply to the right above the gorge, and hereabouts a rocky buff, known as the Study, commands a remarkable view of the whole scene.

Imagine you are standing on this belvedere and gazing upon a scene which might have been one of Nature's primeval workshops. On your left, the three great spurs of Bidean—Beinn Fhada, Gearr Aonach and Aonach Dubh—follow almost parallel lines as they rise into the sky and appear to overhang the glen far below. Your eye skims up these bold cliffs and is inevitably led along their ridges to rest finally upon the lovely peak of Stob Coire nan Lochan, which hides the real summit of the mountain. On your right the great ridge of Aonach Eagach sweeps round in a gigantic curve, its black forbidding pinnacles and stone-swept gullies following one another to end at Sgòr nam Fiannaidh, the sentinel at the foot of the glen. Three thousand feet below, the thin line of the road winds round at the base of these tottering masses, and as you advance along it you imagine they may fall and overwhelm you. When you approach the gloomy waters of the loch you will perceive Ossian's Cave high up on the left in the face of Aonach Dubh, and then you will come to the bridge over the Coe where the road bifurcates. The left branch carries the heavy traffic to Lower Glencoe, while that on the right leads to Clachaig and eventually to Loch Leven.

BEN DOURAN FROM LOCH TULLA

THE BLACKMOUNT FROM QUEENSHOUSE, RANNOCH MOOR

BUACHAILLE ETIVE MÒR FROM KINGSHOUSE

GLENCOE FROM THE STUDY

AONACH DUBH FROM CLACHAIG

BIDEAN NAM BIAN

BIDEAN NAM BIAN is the highest of nine tops which rise from the mountain range of the same name to the south of Glencoe, and is the crowning peak of Argyllshire. Its well-known buttresses overhanging the glen, together with An t'Sròn facing Clachaig, are surmounted by fine ridges, all of which culminate at the cairn on the summit. These spurs enclose three magnificent corries which give access to the ridges, and two of them also to the reigning peak. They contain many fine crags which provide sport for the rock climber. Two of these—the Diamond and Church Door Buttresses—are well seen from the bridge over the Coe where the old and new roads meet.

Bidean nam Bian is famous among mountaineers for its magnificent ridge walks, all of which may be undertaken without difficulty. The quickest way to the summit from Clachaig is either by way of An t'Sròn, whose gully is such a prominent feature when seen from the west, and then over the high ridge commencing with Stob Coire nam Beith, or by threading the corrie on the left of this top, and attaining the summit directly up the scree slopes from its further reaches. Those who follow these routes, however, miss much of the grandeur of the range, and it is better to ascend one of the Three Sisters, traverse the ridges, taking in Bidean on the way, and descend by one of the above routes. The longest of these 'walks' is from Beinn Fhada to An t'Sròn, and if a lift can be obtained from Clachaig to the Study, it may be easily accomplished in a day. If no transport is available, however, it is better to scale Aonach Dubh and thus shorten the circuit considerably.

The grand western façade of this mountain always beckons irresistibly to the climber staying at Clachaig, and he would not be ill-advised to make this his first objective. It may be ascended more directly by the Dinner Time Buttress, which is clearly seen between the well-defined gullies on either side of it. This affords a good scramble, as does also the ascent of its northern face leading up to the shelf below Ossian's Cave, and both courses end just below the summit cairn. The view from this isolated belvedere is indeed one of the most striking in all Scotland, because it provides three entirely different scenes, all of which will for ever appeal to the mountaineer.

When you set foot on the summit, your gaze is arrested by the lovely lines of Stob Coire nan Lochan, and if the peak is clad in snow, it will make an unforgettable picture, with its glittering garment descending into the corrie far below, and the naked rock buttresses supporting the north ridge adding considerably to its stature. You will then turn to look down into Lower Glencoe, where Clachaig now appears as a white spot on the vast landscape spread out at your feet. Your eye will sweep across the glimmering waters of Lochs Leven and Linnhe to rest finally upon the shadowy hills forming the western horizon. You will then turn inevitably to look northwards across the abysmal depths of the narrower reaches of the glen, where Aonach Eagach rises for 3,000 feet in one dynamic sweep from the road. Its dark, gullied precipices present a grim and forbidding aspect and are surmounted by a pinnacled ridge whose appearance from this unsurpassed viewpoint will hold you spellbound. You will wish to dally over this marvellous panorama, but as you still have a long way to go, you had better turn your steps in the direction of Stob Coire nan Lochan and scale the northern ridge to its summit. Here the vista to the north is superb, for you now look over Aonach Eagach to the Lochaber Hills where the snowy crest of Ben Nevis rises into the sky to dominate the mountain scene. To the south, the two supporting buttresses of Bidean make a grand picture high above the corrie, and you will traverse the narrow ridge surmounting them which connects your viewpoint with Bidean. It is only a short scramble to the summit of the mountain, and here you will gaze in admiration upon the wide panorama unfolded in all directions. A grand array of peaks greets you whichever way you look, and for the first time on this expedition you will perceive Ben Cruachan rising into the sky to the south beyond the glistening waters of Loch Etive.

A high ridge connects Bidean with Stob Coire nam Beith, and you will saunter along it entranced by the views in every direction. When you have descended some little distance from the reigning peak you will linger to admire its Alpine appearance, and when you stand on the summit of its western sentinel you will obtain an unrestricted view to the north, where the monarch of Britain's mountains dominates the horizon and the snow-capped peaks of the Northern Highlands fade into the dim distance to its left.

The descent to Clachaig is interesting, with a close prospect of the grand crags of Stob Coire nam Beith on your right and a peep into the recesses of the corrie when you come down to its lip from An t'Sròn. You follow the burn down to the bridge over the Coe and thus complete one of the finest ridge traverses in all Scotland.

THE SUMMIT OF BIDEAN NAM BIAN FROM THE WEST

LOOKING ACROSS GLENCOE T

AONACH EAGACH FROM AONACH DUBH

AONACH EAGACH

AONACH EAGACH forms the north wall of Glencoe and stretches for over five miles from the Devil's Staircase in the east to the Pap of Glencoe in the west. Known also as the Notched Ridge on account of the deep indentations of its crest, it provides the climber with one of the most sensational traverses on the mainland of Scotland, and indeed in the whole of Britain. The ridge is fairly broad from its eastern end to Sròn Garbh, and it then contracts slightly as far as Am Bodach, where the narrowest section begins. From here to Stob Coire Lèith it is characterised by an array of tottering pinnacles, separated from each other by giddy *arêtes*, below which stone-swept gullies fall precipitously to the south into Glencoe some 3,000 feet below, and to the north towards Kinlochleven. The ridge broadens again at Stob Coire Lèith, and after passing Sgòr nam Fiannaidh swings round to the north-west and ends at the Pap of Glencoe overlooking the lower stretches of Loch Leven.

Seen from the River Coe near Clachaig on a sunny afternoon, with fine clouds drifting overhead in a purple sky, Aonach Eagach looks strangely beautiful in spite of its shattered appearance, but when the mists drift across its mighty crest and the pinnacles pop in and out of the cloud, this aspect changes to one of grim and savage melancholy, and the solitary climber who has crossed its ghostly spires is glad to be safely back in his lodgings.

The traverse of the Notched Ridge may be effected in either direction, and it is a matter of opinion which is the more fascinating. The quickest way to see the best part of it is to ascend Am Bodach from the cottage of Altnareigh, which faces Gearr Aonach across the glen, and to descend by the stone shoot coming down on the south side from the col below Stob Coire Lèith. I had heard and read many sensational stories of the walk over Aonach Eagach, and as this was the first occasion on which I had had the opportunity to test them, I looked forward to the traverse with considerable interest, and as I was alone, with some trepidation.

Climbing steadily from the Study on a cold April morning I was entranced by the magnificent spectacle of Bidean nam Bian across the glen, which from an altitude of about 2,000 feet afforded a wonderful picture of mountain architecture, with the higher ridges covered with snow and Stob Coire nan Lochan taking precedence over Bidean for nobility of form and outline. Soon after midday I was standing by the cairn on Am Bodach and looking along the crest towards Meall Dearg, the highest top on the narrowest part of the ridge. Below me vast precipices swept down into Glencoe, intersected on my right by a fearsome gully which is a feature of the mountain when observed from the glen. There is a considerable drop to the ridge from Am Bodach, and I was soon descending the buttress leading down to it, and afterwards traversed the pinnacles without much difficulty as far as Meall Dearg. This is a magnificent viewpoint for the appraisal of the finest section, where the shattered pinnacles follow one another so closely along the ridge as to suggest an almost continuous *arête*.

From afar these obstacles looked unsurmountable, but I found on tackling them that they were easier than I had supposed, and in a short time I had reached the Crazy Pinnacles. These well-known features of Aonach Eagach stand precariously at the top of gullies which sweep down either side of the mountain, and the wind shrieked through the gap in wild anger as I passed them. Looking back from here, you see a great isolated pinnacle rise from the ridge with the cairn of Meall Dearg looming grimly on the skyline to the left, while above the first of the Crazy Pinnacles there is a glimpse of Loch Eilde Mòr reposing amid the dim shadowy hills to the north-east. I climbed the short chimney which emerges at the top of another pinnacle and from it I looked down into the abysmal depths of Glencoe, where the rippling waters of Loch Triochatan caught the level afternoon sunlight. One pinnacle followed another in this contorted line of obstacles until quite suddenly, and to my surprise, I climbed down the last one and all the fun and speculation was over. I passed the stone shoot on the col and was soon standing on Stob Coire Lèith, but the walk seemed less fascinating after the excitement of the narrow traverse. As I advanced along the broad grassy ridge towards Sgòr nam Fiannaidh, the Pap of Glencoe presented a less imposing appearance and partially blocked the wide western panorama of loch and ben stretching away beneath the opalescent sky to the sea. Far below on my left I perceived the bridge over the Coe, now a toy in a vast landscape, and I hastened down towards it.

Aonach Eagach had been grand fun after all, and nothing like so difficult as I had been led to believe; in fact, it had proved to be another magnificent and perhaps unique Highland ridge walk—and one that should be undertaken by all mountaineers.

AONACH EAGACH FROM GLENCOE

BIDEAN NAM BIAN FROM AONACH EAGACH

AONACH EAGACH LOOKING EAST FROM THE CRAZY PINNACLES

BALLACHULISH AND BEN VARE

BALLACHULISH is familiar to thousands of tourists who have spent motoring holidays in the Highlands; the mere mention of the name will perhaps recall their crossing the Ferry here to save many miles of detour by way of Kinlochleven.

The village stands well back from Loch Linnhe and faces northwards across Loch Leven, but unhappily the quarry workings have spoilt any romantic setting it ever had, and the lover of nature associates the name with the hotels at the Ferry rather than with the houses a couple of miles to the east. The situation is delightful, and together with Onich to the north is reminiscent of parts of the Riviera. To the south it is enclosed by the steep wooded escarpments of the Ben Vare Range, while to the west, the magnificent hills of Ardgour, crowned by Garbh Bheinn, form a wonderful skyline across the rippling waters of Loch Linnhe. The view to the north is rather shut in, but the vista to the east makes a characteristic Highland picture in which the Glencoe Bastions rise into the sky and the Pap of Glencoe is a conspicuous feature. This encircling combination of loch and ben should in itself be sufficient to charm the visitor, but it is at sundown on a favourable day that the real glory of the scene is revealed. On such occasions the marvellous colourings of the heavens, seen above the black outline of the western hills across the loch and reflected in its glittering waters, provide a canvas which has to be seen to be believed.

The environs of Loch Leven are observed to best advantage from its northern shore, where the lake makes a charming foreground to the hills beyond. There is a little bay close to the Ferry, and I have often lingered here to admire the mystic lights and shadows on Sgòrr Dhonuill, which rises at the head of the deep glen to the south. The vista towards Glencoe is better, too, because the more open viewpoint displays these mountains to greater advantage.

When the lover of the hills stays in Ballachulich he is usually there to climb Ben Vare, and although the walk over this gigantic horseshoe occupies a long day it presents no difficulties, and the views from the great summit ridge are some of the finest in Scotland. The circuit may be made in either direction, but I have a preference for the east-west route because the lighting is then more favourable. It is impossible to see the topography of the range from the vicinity of the hotels since the spurs are so steep and tower above the road, but from the low hills to the north of Loch Leven a more comprehensive prospect is obtained, and the three tops, together with the glens far below, are more clearly defined.

Spring is one of the best times to scale Ben Vare (spelt Beinn a Bheithir), because its snow-clad tops add much to the interest of the walk. A path leaves the road near the church and follows the burn to the open ground above the trees. Sgòrr Dhearg rises above the corrie ahead, but instead of entering it you climb the slopes on the left giving access to the ridge which leads to Sgòrr Bhan, the eastern top of the range. This subsidiary peak is well placed for viewing the beautiful curve of the ridge rising to the summit of the mountain, and when seen under favourable conditions it is one of the loveliest sights in the district.

Sgòrr Dhearg is the highest top in the Ben Vare Horseshoe, and as such commands extensive prospects on all sides. The Lochaber Hills are seen to cover an enormous area to the north of Loch Leven, and appear above the ridge you have ascended. The Bastions of Glencoe crowd up the landscape to the east and Bidean is not observed to advantage from this viewpoint. The most striking vista is to the west, where the summit ridge falls to the bealach and then rises steeply to Sgòrr Dhonuill, the next top to be climbed in this walk. It is only 800 feet from the col to the summit, but this is a stiff ascent, and when you reach the cairn you will sit down and rest while admiring the more open view to the west, where the hills of Ardgour fade away into the distance beyond Loch Linnhe.

There is a glimpse of the narrow exit of Loch Leven to the north across the flanks of Sgòrr a'Chaolais, the little horn-shaped peak when seen from below, while to the left the ridge opens out into a broad plateau which swings round in a great curve to end at Creag Ghorm, the spur high above the hotels at Ballachulish. There are several attractive lochans sprinkled about on this arm of the horseshoe, and to traverse it is a much longer walk than you may suppose, because there are so many hidden ravines which have to be crossed or circumvented before the cairn is reached.

The direct descent from this point is steep and the lower flanks of the hill are closely planted with spruce. It is better, therefore, either to go down on the western side towards Kentallen or to find a route about halfway along into Gleann a'Chaolais and thus back to Ballachulish.

SUNSET FROM BALLACHULISH

BEN VARE FROM ABOVE LOCH LEVEN

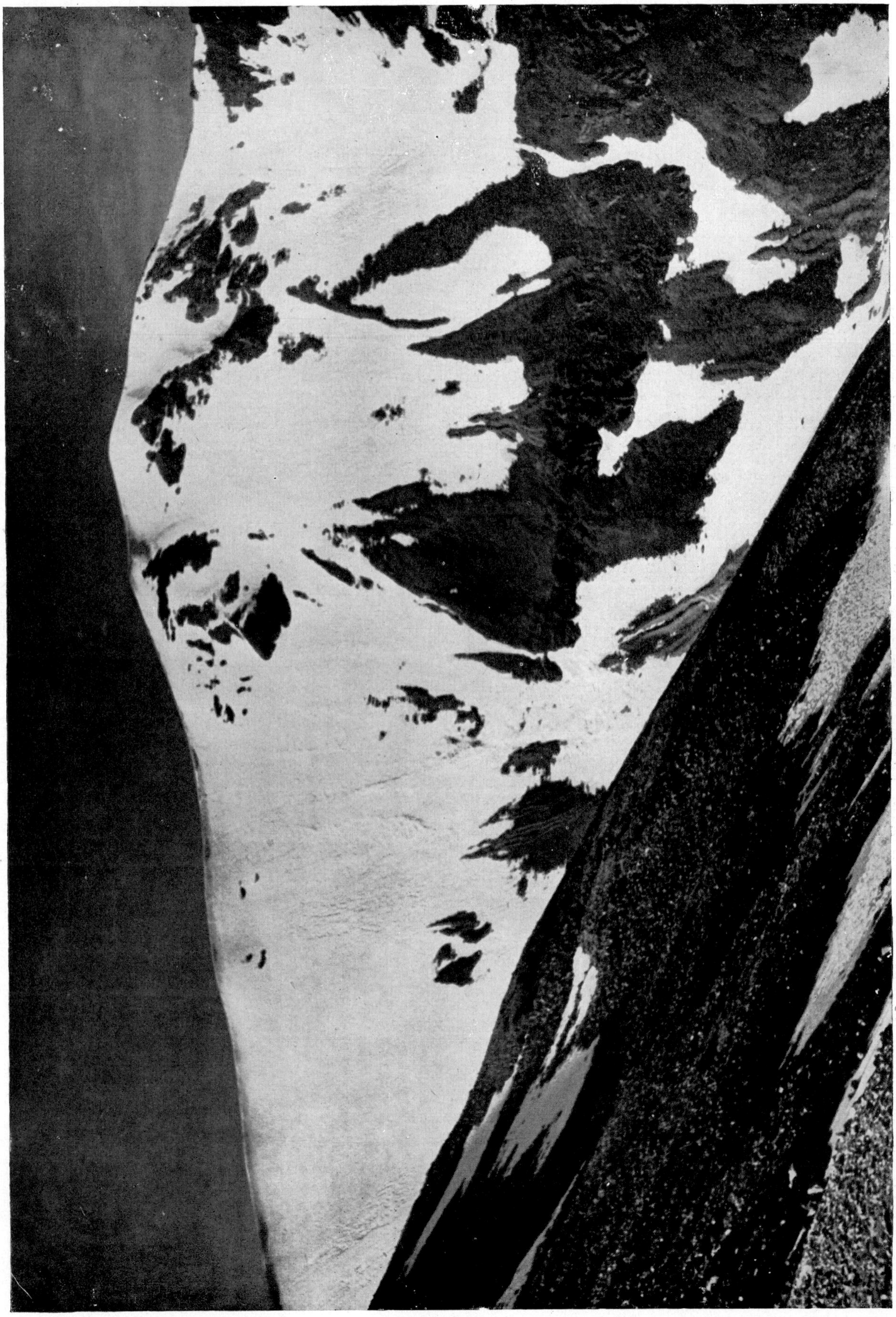

SGÒRR DHEARG FROM THE SLOPES OF BEINN BHAN

GLEN NEVIS AND THE MAMORES

FORT WILLIAM overlooks the head waters of Loch Linnhe and is well placed for the exploration of the western section of the Lochaber Hills. Roads radiate from the town along most of the principal glens, and it is also served by the West Highland Railway from Glasgow, the line continuing westwards to Mallaig whence the steamer conveys passengers to Skye.

The easiest walk in the vicinity is to Glen Nevis, where a road gives access to the wild reaches of the valley and ends near the Gorge. A stony track then leads into the hills and ultimately emerges at Loch Treig. The glen is a long one; the road, extending for only seven miles from Fort William, is about half its total length. There are three well-defined sections; the first is of a pastoral character as far as the cottages at Polldubh, the second stretches from this hamlet to Steall, where the scenery is raised from the commonplace to the sublime in the vicinity of the gorge, while the third threads the open moorland between the Aonachs on the north and the Mamores on the south.

I have walked through Glen Nevis several times, and with one exception I have always been unlucky with the weather and have returned to Fort William wet to the skin. Although the way is long I think it is more interesting to go through the glen on foot rather than to ride in a car, whereas a car is indispensable if the ascent of any of the peaks of the Mamores is included in the itinerary.

You leave the main road at the northern end of the town and follow the south bank of the river. This skirts Cow Hill and then turns to the south, when the glen opens up with grand views ahead of Stob Bàn and Sgùrr a'Mhaim, two prominent peaks of the Mamores. The glen is shut in to the east by the steep flanks of Ben Nevis, where the tourist track ascends from Achintee, and on the west by the outliers of Mullach nan Coirean, the eastern sentinel of the group. The road bends sharply to the east at Polldubh and crosses a bridge over an attractive waterfall, with splendid views of the wild section of the glen ahead. It meanders across the lower slopes of Càrn Dearg, with many a lovely glimpse of the stream on the right cascading through miniature ravines of great beauty. It ends at the foot of Meall Cumhann, and you continue into the gorge by way of a stony track which rises precariously at some considerable height above the river. The vista to the south is magnificent, and perhaps one of the best known in the Highlands. Ahead of you the fine peak of An Gearanach rises above the gorge, where the torrent passes through a narrow cleft in the hills and sparkles in the sunlight as it disappears into a ravine at your feet. If the weather has been wet you will easily perceive the great Steall Waterfall emerging from Coire a'Mhail to fall several hundred feet over the bare crags on the right of An Gearanach. The cottages of Steall are situated beyond the gorge, but at the top a swing bridge spans the torrent and gives access to one of them. The other stands on the open moorland farther to the east, where the scenery is commonplace.

The Mamore Forest is a long range of hills stretching from east to west for about seven miles, and enclosing Glen Nevis on the south. It comprises sixteen well-defined tops which are connected by high ridges, and provides the mountaineer with some of the finest ridge-wandering in the Highlands. Binnein Mòr is the highest peak in the group and may be ascended from Kinlochleven, which town is also a good centre for several of the peaks as far west as Stob Bàn. The western section is accessible from Fort William and especially from Polldubh, where a well-defined track leads into the deep recesses of Coire nam Mhusgain to the south and ultimately rises to the saddle between Stob Bàn and Sgòr an Iubhair.

The best viewpoint for the appraisal of the group is undoubtedly Sgùrr a'Mhaim, which is the second highest peak and stands in isolation well to the north of the others. It is connected with them by a narrow escarpment known as the Devil's Ridge, the vast slopes on either side of which fall precipitously into the great corries dropping into Glen Nevis. The view to the west from here is one of the most magnificent in the district, and reveals the three great buttresses supporting the conical top of Stob Bàn, together with the ridges stretching away to the west and ending at Mullach nan Coirean.

Sgùrr a'Mhaim has a cup-shaped corrie to the north of the summit, and this is a conspicuous feature of the view to the south from Càrn Mòr Dearg. The famous Arête connecting the latter with Ben Nevis is well seen from this peak, which reveals almost the full height of the 4,000-feet slopes falling from the Ben into Glen Nevis far below. The prospect of the Eastern Mamores is also comprehensive, with Binnein Mòr rising at the end of the chain. Mullach nan Coirean may be climbed from the old road between Fort William and Kinlochleven, and commands splendid vistas of the narrow undulating ridges which characterise the whole group.

THE WILDS OF GLEN NEVIS FROM POLLDUBH

IN GLEN NEVIS

AN GEARANACH AND THE STEALL WATERFALL FROM THE GORGE OF GLEN NEVIS

STOB BÀN AND THE WESTERN MAMORE

IDGES FROM THE DEVIL'S RIDGE

BEN NEVIS

BEN NEVIS reaches a height of 4,406 feet and is the most lofty peak in Britain. It rises to the east of Fort William, but the view of it from the town is obscured by the outlying spur of Meall a t'Suidhe. The vast bulk of the mountain is well seen from the western shore of Loch Linnhe, but better still from the hills behind Banavie, when the magnificent ridges and buttresses enclosing the north-east corrie are revealed rising from the Glen Allt a'Mhuilinn, which separates the Ben from Càrn Mòr Dearg.

A broad and well-defined path ascends the western slopes of Ben Nevis from Achintee, a farm easily reached by road from Fort William. It goes round the flanks of Meall a t'Suidhe and passes the small lochan lying to the east of this top before bending sharply to the right towards the old Half-Way House. Thereafter it zigzags up the stony declivities of the mountain and emerges on the summit plateau near the exit from Coire na Ciste. It then follows the long line of cliffs and ends at the ruin of the Observatory, where a series of cairns mark the route taken by the late occupants in bad weather. This path is well known to thousands of tourists, but it is a strenuous climb and bereft of interest until the plateau is reached. The mountaineer will not scorn this track for his descent late in the day, but he will seldom scale the Ben by it, preferring the longer and infinitely more interesting ascent by Càrn Mòr Dearg, where the well-known Arête connects this peak with the north-eastern cairn of the plateau.

You leave the main road near Lochy Bridge and follow a path through the grounds of the distillery which crosses the railway and gives access to the moor. It is a stiff walk by the burn up to the wide strath at the entrance to the Glen Allt a'Mhuilinn, where you pick your way carefully across the bog and afterwards ascend the stony slopes to the left which end at Càrn Beag Dearg. This is the northern sentinel of the mile-long ridge rising to Càrn Mòr Dearg, and the view from it of the intermediate top of Càrn Dearg Meadhonach is very fine, with snow-clad slopes falling into the glen on the left and the black forbidding pinnacles of the subsidiary ridge imparting a grim touch to the scene. As you advance along the crest the panorama to the right across the Glen Allt a'Mhuilinn is wonderfully impressive, with the magnificent twin ridges supporting the summit of Ben Nevis and the snow-plastered mural precipices encircling Coire na Ciste between it and Càrn Dearg. The Great Buttress of this outlier towers into the sky nearly 2,000 feet above the S.M.C. Hut, which from your high viewpoint looks diminutive and perched precariously on a crag near the burn far below. The vista from Càrn Dearg Meadhonach is finer still because it reveals the lovely pyramid of Càrn Mòr Dearg as well as the vast panorama to the west.

You will hasten to ascend this shapely peak, and on reaching the summit will gaze in admiration upon the famous Arête, the narrow undulating crest of which sweeps round in a great curve to join the Ben on your right. To the south you will look beyond the first excrescence on the Arête to the shadowy outlines of the Mamore peaks, which loom through the haze above the abysmal depths of Glen Nevis far below. The panorama is superb, and unsurpassed in Britain, and if perchance you are a solitary climber you may perceive no sign of life in any direction—in fact you might imagine yourself to be the last living person on earth. You will doubtless linger on this unrivalled belvedere until the cold wind compels you to move, when you will plunge down the slopes and begin the traverse of the Arête. This is a delightful scramble, and when you reach its lowest point you may look back along the ridge to Càrn Mòr Dearg, where Aonach Mòr rises in the background. There is still nearly one thousand feet of ascent to the summit of the Ben, and a steady climb over the snow will lead you to the north-eastern extremity of the plateau. A short walk along the crest of the precipices reveals the cairn, together with the ruin of the Observatory.

On a good day the panorama from the summit of Ben Nevis is one of the finest in the country, and comprises innumerable snow-capped peaks fading away into the distance in all directions. The most arresting feature, however, is the prospect to the north across the great snow cornices overhanging the terrific precipices which enclose the corrie. On your left these are split by the fearsome Gardyloo Gully, in the vicinity of which a realistic picture of the summit is obtained. You follow the long line of cliffs, where every type of snow and rock architecture is arrayed fantastically on your right. The sublime sweep of the snow above the gullies may appeal to you, or perhaps your gaze will be attracted by the naked rocks of the Tower, which may be examined in perfect safety either from above or from below. You will amble slowly down the gentle slopes of the plateau until you reach the exit from Coire na Ciste, where the path, perhaps now hidden by a great snowfield, leads down by the Red Burn to Achintee.

THE SUMMIT CLIFFS OF BEN NEVIS

THE PRECIPICES OF BEN NEVIS FROM CÀRN MÒR DEARG

COIRE NA CISTE AND THE BUTTRESSES OF CÀRN DEARG

SNOWDONIA

THIS is the name usually given to the North Wales mountains enclosed on the east by the Conway Valley and on the south by Tremadoc Bay. The range covers a relatively small area, being about twenty-five miles long from north to south and some twelve miles broad. The district comprises five well-defined groups of hills, each separated from the others by valleys along which excellent roads have been driven. One of these is the important link between London and Ireland, the Holyhead Road, which is also the principal means of access to the district itself, reaching it at Bettws-y-Coed. A railway connecting Bettws with Llandudno Junction is a convenient approach for those coming from London or the Midlands. The hill country may be entered also from the south, but the route is more sinuous and is used only by those living in the west country.

The five mountain groups forming Snowdonia are as follows:

1.—The Carnedds lie to the north of the Holyhead Road between Capel Curig and Bethesda, and extend almost as far as the sea. They are not characterised by any well-defined peaks, but consist mainly of rounded hills connected by broad high ridges and covered with grass on their southern flanks. On the north, however, they present a wilder aspect, and some of the cwms are remarkable for their outcrops of rock, all of which are some distance from the main road.

2.—The Glyders are situated between the Ogwen and Llanberis Valleys. They are noted for the strange rock formations to be found on the long summit ridge and include the isolated mountain of Tryfan, the most shapely peak in the district. In addition to these well-known features the Glyders enclose Cwm Idwal, one of the finest mountain hollows in the country. It lies so near the highway at Ogwen Cottage that it can be reached by the pedestrian in about a quarter of an hour.

3.—The Snowdon group rises to the south of the Llanberis Pass and is bounded on the other side by the Colwyn Valley. It is crowned by Y Wyddfa, the highest peak in Wales, contains three cwms renowned for their magnificent rock architecture, and includes also the Horseshoe, a ridge which for scale and superb rock structure is unsurpassed in the whole of Britain.

4.—The Moel Hebog group lies to the south-west of Snowdon and extends almost as far as Carnarvon Bay. It is relatively inaccessible excepting from Beddgelert, and consists mainly of rounded grassy hills of which the most interesting feature is the long narrow ridge to the south of the Nantlle Valley.

5.—The Moel Siabod group lies to the south-east of the others and occupies a large area between Capel Curig in the north and Portmadoc in the south. Seen from certain viewpoints it exhibits two shapely peaks, Cnicht and Moel Siabod itself. Numerous small lakes are spread about the group, many of them at high levels, and they provide good sport for the angler. The hills are covered largely with grass and heather, but the higher parts reveal intermittent stretches of broken rock.

The mountains of Snowdonia are noted for their sombre magnificence, and have attracted much attention since Pennant wrote an account of them in 1781. Many fine peaks grace these hills and a few of them display shapely lines when seen from advantageous viewpoints. Tryfan, as I have said, is possibly the most beautiful, its forlorn aspect from the east appealing strongly to all mountaineers. By morning light the three fine buttresses supporting its summit are seen to advantage, and in snow it assumes all the splendour of an Alpine peak. Snowdon is majestic when viewed from the shore of Llyn Llydaw, although from the west it loses much of its grandeur and appears as the apex of a number of great high pendent ridges. Crib Goch is no less beautiful when observed from Pen-y-Pass, and Lliwedd also presents an impressive appearance, with its great precipices falling steeply to the scree slopes above Llyn Llydaw. Carnedd Llewelyn is one of the giants of Snowdonia and the highest top in the most northern group. The summit is of Byzantine rather than of Gothic form and covers a great area which is subject to the most misty conditions in the district. Cnicht is of such proportions when seen from the south as to be often described as the Welsh Matterhorn, but from every other angle it appears as a long, insignificant slaty ridge. Even Moel Siabod presents a fine pyramidal outline from the same direction in spite of its somewhat bulky appearance from all other angles. The Moel Hebog group contains numerous rounded hills, but Y Garn II, standing at the entrance to the Nantlle valley, attracts much attention by its savage appearance from the east.

There are four cwms in Snowdonia which exemplify some of our grandest rock architecture, and as such are the resort of the rock climber. Cwm Dyli is of gigantic proportions, Cwms Idwal and Brwynog compete with it for magnificence, while Cwm Glas is smaller and famed for its Alpine flora, which has attracted botanists of world repute.

The valleys of Snowdonia have often a grim and forbidding aspect, but a few of them are adorned with trees which provide a softer and more appealing prospect, especially when seen in the spring. For instance, the Vale of Gwynant possesses great charm, its trees canopying the road and the shores of its lakes, while rhododendrons add a note of colour. In the vicinity of Bettws-y-Coed both the Llugwy and Lledr valleys are well wooded and very picturesque, the banks of the rivers providing many a lovely vista. The district is, however, famous for the wilder type of scenery, of which the Llanberis Pass is the finest example. Here the rugged hills with their beetling bastions frown down on the narrow road, and when the weather is stormy the valley assumes an atmosphere of sinister gloom.

The lakes are the least attractive feature of the Snowdon landscape. With a few exceptions they have a barren setting, and become picturesque only when illuminated by some freak of lighting. Some of the smaller lakes, however, have great charm, especially in the autumn when the tufts of heather, set amid the stooks of rock fringing their shores, add a purple daintiness to the scene.

The Snowdon group affords one of the finest examples of scale in the country. Here the famous Horseshoe encloses Cwm Dyli, where the savage cliffs and giddy precipices frown down on the lake far below and the crest of the engirdling hills undulates in one magnificent sweep from Crib Goch to Lliwedd. Nature has excelled here in the creation of one of her grandest scenes, in which the proportions are so perfectly contrived that the newcomer is usually deceived by their size. From the summit cairn of Crib Goch the view is a wonderful example of sublime mountain form.

The weather in Snowdonia is subject to the usual vagaries of all hill country adjacent to the Atlantic. South-west winds prevail with the formation of cloud about Y Wyddfa and eventual precipitation, especially on the leeward side where Cwm Dyli has the highest rainfall in the neighbourhood. The brightest conditions are experienced in the spring, and this period offers less chance of disappointment to those who wish to wander along the ridges and enjoy the fine panoramas. In winter, and particularly in February, the splendour of Snowdonia reaches its peak. At that time snow transforms many of the hills into magnificent Alpine giants, and the Snowdon group itself, when seen under these conditions from Capel Curig, undoubtedly makes the most superb mountain landscape in the country.

Snowdonia has many good centres from which the district may be explored, and the accommodation there is all the visitor could wish. It is possible to stay in Capel Curig and by using a car be at the foot of any hill early enough in the day to allow ample time to climb it and be back for dinner. Pen-y-Pass and Pen-y-Gwryd are the most centrally situated for all the groups excepting the Carnedds, and Pen-y-Pass has the advantage of standing in the very shadow of the great hills and at such an altitude as to save over 1,000 feet in the neighbouring ascents.

The finest impression of these mountains is obtained by approaching them from Bettws-y-Coed, walking first over the outer groups, then the Glyders and finally over Snowdon itself. In a fortnight much of their grandeur may be seen if the weather is propitious. The district offers ample opportunity for the enjoyment of rock climbing, which varies from the easier courses—such as the Milestone Buttress and Idwal Slabs—to the severe ascents of Lliwedd and Clogwyn D'ur-arddu.

SNOWDON FROM THE ROYAL BRIDGE—CAPEL

SNOWDON FRO

HE CAPEL LAKES

CAPEL CURIG AND THE OGWEN VALLEY

CAPEL CURIG is a straggling village extending for about a mile along the Holyhead Road, from the bridge near Cyfyng Falls to its junction with the highway leading to the left to Pen-y-Gwryd. The houses are picturesquely situated in a long twisting valley which is narrow in places and more open in others. Woods canopy the lower slopes and are threaded with paths which provide the less active visitor with many a pleasant walk, while the village contains several good hotels which make it an excellent centre for the exploration of the district.

The Pinnacles of Capel Curig rise immediately behind the Bryn Tyrch Hotel, but are not noticed in the walk westwards through the village. From the stream beyond, however, the three craggy eminences make a charming picture, and provide the climber with some amusement on an 'off' day. This viewpoint is close to the Royal Hotel, which dates back to 1801, and occupies one of the finest positions in the country. It overlooks the Llynau Mymbyr, where the Snowdon group rises into the western sky some seven miles away, and constitutes the most superb mountain landscape in Britain.

Moel Siabod is Capel's own mountain: its summit is seen above the dwarf oaks fringing the river in the wider section of the valley. The peak, however, is best observed from the vicinity of the Ugly House. On one occasion when I saw it, a late winter afternoon, the eastern ridges were iced and looked almost Himalayan as they glittered in the setting sun, while cloud drifted over the summit ridge from the west. The usual ascent is from the bridge spanning the torrent which emerges from the twin lakes. It is an easy walk up the grassy slopes, which in their higher reaches give place to rock, and from there it is an interesting scramble along the crest to the cairn. The more attractive approach, however, is by way of the eastern façade, where Llyn y Foel reposes at the foot of the precipices and where a fine shattered ridge rises directly to the cairn. The view from the summit is extensive, but the Snowdon Group looks less impressive from this high belvedere. The most remarkable feature in the wide landscape is Tryfan, whose three magnificent buttresses rise in splendid isolation above the intervening ridge of the Glyders.

Llyn Crafnant is a pleasant walk from Capel Curig, where the path leaves the road near the church. It zigzags across the gently swelling moorland, and after passing Clogwyn Mawr on the left enters a picturesque gorge, beyond which the lake is revealed far below and set in a fine amphitheatre of craggy hills.

The Ogwen Valley stretches westwards from Capel Curig to the foot of Llyn Ogwen, and thereafter continues as Nant Ffrancon in a north-westerly direction as far as Bethesda. It is the dividing line between the Carnedds in the north and the Glyders in the south, and from it the many fine rock formations of the Glyders are well seen. It is agreeable enough to walk on the wide grass verge of the Holyhead Road all the way to Ogwen Cottage, but much pleasanter to follow the course of the Afon Llugwy, or better still to amble along the old grass track in the very shadow of the hills. These routes converge, however, before the north ridge of Tryfan is encountered, and the remaining section is completed along the road which skirts the southern shore of Llyn Ogwen.

Tryfan is a favourite mountain of many rock climbers, who often stay at Helyg, a comfortable hut owned by the members of the Climbers' Club, and which stands south of the main road. The peak has three magnificent rock buttresses which rise from Heather Terrace to support the shapely summit. Here two naked rocks known as Adam and Eve stand side by side, and are conspicuous features replacing the more usual cairn. The ascent of either Heather Terrace or the North Ridge presents no difficulties, but the latter is an excellent scramble in its higher reaches, and there are one or two sensational places where Llyn Ogwen appears nearly two thousand feet below.

The road skirts the base of the North Ridge of Tryfan. The rippling waters of Llyn Ogwen appear ahead, and just round the corner at the tenth milestone from Bangor, the popular Milestone Buttress rises above the road. Ogwen Cottage nestles below a rocky bluff at the foot of the lake where the steep shattered cliffs of Pen yr Oleuwen rise to the north, almost from its very doors.

Cwm Idwal is only a short walk from the Cottage, and on arriving at the foot of Llyn Idwal, which reposes in its rocky bosom, you see the magnificent engirdling crags to the south. A track leads round the shores of the lake, but that on the east is much worn by the thousands of scramblers who have followed it to Idwal Slabs, another source of enjoyment for the tyro. The superb rock amphitheatre beyond the lake will immediately arrest the gaze of the mountaineer, whose eye will skim across the glimmering waters at his feet and follow the boulder-strewn slopes beyond, to rest finally on the Devil's Kitchen, a great chasm splitting the face of the crags.

THE EASTERN FACE OF TRYFAN

LLYN OGWEN FROM THE MILESTONE BUTTRESS

THE DEVIL'S KITCHEN FROM LLYN IDWAL

THE CARNEDDS

THIS group of hills occupies a vast area to the north of the Holyhead Road, and its flanks extend almost as far as Conway Bay. It is remarkable for its broad high ridges, which culminate in Carnedd Llewelyn, the third highest peak in Snowdonia, and also for its many wild valleys which often end with a fine display of bold crags. A number of lakes of varying size are sprinkled about the south-eastern recesses of the group, but some of them are so remote as to be seldom visited. The range is eminently suitable for ridge wandering, but is notorious for the sudden appearance of mist on the high tops, so that all pedestrians frequenting these places would be well advised to carry both map and compass.

Capel Curig and Ogwen Cottage are well situated for the exploration of the Carnedds, and while it is possible to walk in one day from the latter over the principal summits as far as Tal y Fan and then down to one of the roads, there are several interesting features in the southern part of this range which would be missed by following such a course. One of the most repaying walks is from Capel to Ogwen by way of Carnedd Llewelyn. You leave the Holyhead Road near Bronheulog and follow the power lines across the boggy moorland to the high ground above the head of Llyn Cowlyd, which lies between the precipitous slopes of Creigiau Gleision on the east and Pen Llithrig on the west. You ascend the steep trackless flanks of the latter, and on reaching the cairn, discover an almost full-length prospect of the group to the north-west, where the Byzantine summit of Carnedd Llewelyn rises to the highest point on the long ridge. A craggy escarpment falls to the west of Pen Llithrig. You descend this and walk up the shaly slopes ahead to the top of Pen Helgi. You may have noticed the grand crags of Craig yr Ysfa falling into Cwm Eigiau on your right, and after passing the cairn on this grassy hill you descend the steep shattered ridge to the col which gives access to its crest.

This is a fascinating place in which to linger on a pleasant day, and you will be enchanted by the close view of the magnificent crags enclosing the Amphitheatre. A fine buttress on the left makes an excellent foreground to the vista into Cwm Eigiau far below. Carnedd Llewelyn looms on the horizon to the north-west and it is an easy walk up to the large cairn crowning its vast summit from which a wide panorama is unfolded in all directions. The most arresting prospect is to the west, where you look beyond many a shapely summit of the Glyders and Snowdon Groups to the sea. At sundown, particularly, this provides a magical and colourful spectacle. You now turn your steps to the south and walk along the airy ridge enclosing Cwm Llafar on the west, where the grim and forbidding crags of Ysgolion Duon fall almost vertically into its head. These precipices are known as the Black Ladders because grassy ledges run horizontally across the dark gullies which seam their face, and from the west they have the appearance of a series of gigantic steps.

Carnedd Dafydd dominates this scene of wild grandeur, and you traverse its summit and descend to the south-west past a number of huge cairns standing amid the maze of boulders which characterise this eminence. You may shorten the route by descending to the left towards the dark waters of Ffynnon Lloer, which lie in a great hollow, and then follow the stream down to Llyn Ogwen. It is far better, however, to continue along the ridge to Pen yr Oleu-wen, which commands unrivalled prospects of the shattered northern face of the Glyders, the grand amphitheatre of Cwm Idwal and the peculiar wedge shape of Tryfan. The climb down to Ogwen Cottage is one of the steepest in the whole of Snowdonia, and if you walk over the ridges in winter you will have to exercise great care when descending the higher reaches.

There are only two climbing courses of importance in the Carnedds—Black Ladders and Craig yr Ysfa—and of these the latter vies in popularity with many others in Snowdonia. It rises at the head of Cwm Eigiau and presents a wonderful appearance by morning light when seen from the floor of this wild valley. It may be conveniently approached from Helyg by a path which undulates across the marshy moorland and passes the dark waters of Ffynnon Llugwy. This lake reposes at the foot of the narrow ridge joining the hills on either side, and it is a good scramble to its top. The descent to the south of Craig yr Ysfa is equally precipitous through the heather and bilberries which cover the hillside. A path then leads round the base of the crags and gives access to all the well-known courses, of which the Great Gully, splitting the northern section of the great cliffs to a height of about 800 feet, is the most fascinating.

Black Ladders may be reached by a circuitous route into Cwm Llafar, but the rotten rocks of this cliff do not encourage frequent visits so that climbers are seldom found there.

CRAIG YR YSFA FROM CWM EIGIAU

THE GWYNANT VALLEY AND CNICHT

NANT GWYNANT is the most picturesque valley in Snowdonia. It rises from Beddgelert in the south to Pen-y-Gwryd in the north, where the road forms a junction with the Llanberis Pass. It is characterised by a number of smallish green straths, in two of which repose delightful lakes, and by several beautifully wooded sections which in the higher reaches give place to the wild open country at the foot of Cwm Dyli. The valley is enclosed on the north by the Snowdon Group and on the south by the long line of hills dominated by Moel Siabod, while a winding road threads its entire length and affords many lovely glimpses of the surrounding hills.

The best way to see this valley is to follow the Afon Glaslyn to its source. Cross the bridge just outside Beddgelert and keep to the path past Dinas Emrys to Llyn Dinas. Skirt its shore and join the road near Nant Gwynant Post Office, beyond which Cwm y Llan opens out on the left. The Watkin Path rises along its wild reaches and is a popular route for the ascent of Y Wyddfa. It passes the late Sir Edward Watkin's chalet, the Gladstone Rock and some disused quarries, and after turning sharply to the right ascends the steep flanks of Lliwedd to emerge at the Pass of the Arrows.

A few houses stand on the right of the road facing Cwm y Llan, and to the north of them a sharp bend suddenly reveals the shimmering waters of Llyn Gwynant some distance below. A boathouse on the opposite shore relieves the general austerity of the scene, which is dominated by the great ridge of Gallt y Wenallt, the terminating escarpment of the Snowdon Horseshoe. The highway follows the southern shore of the lake and on the left reveals the pyramidal top of Yr Aran, a southern outlier of the Snowdon Group. Ahead the Glyders form the horizon, and the steep slopes of the Moel Siabod Group completely shut out the view to the right. Just beyond the head of the lake the road bifurcates, the old one branching off to the left and the new highway rising along the flanks of the hills to the east. It is possible to cross over to the river which now flows on the other side of the valley, but since the views from it are less interesting it is better to walk up the old road to its northern junction. At this point there is a fine prospect of the Snowdon Horseshoe to the left, which encircles the horizon high above Cwm Dyli. Better views of this well-known ridge may be obtained by climbing the hill on the right, and it is then only a short step to Pen-y-Gwryd.

Cnicht is one of the sentinels standing at the southern terminus of the Moel Siabod group, and is a long ridge which falls steeply on the north of Cwm Creosor. Seen from the south it looks very attractive and is known as the Welsh Matterhorn, but from all other directions it is uninteresting.

The long series of hills dominated by Moel Siabod are, for some unknown reason, the least popular in Snowdonia. The high ground at their southern extremity is well sprinkled with many lovely small lakes, so that the group is worthy of much greater attention by all those pedestrians who seek solitude together with fine and interesting viewpoints. One of the finest is Cnicht, where you look down into the abysmal depths of Cwm Creosor, which seem greater than they really are owing to the perfect scale of their surroundings. The rounded summit of Moelwyn Mawr rises to the south-east, and on its left you will observe many of the small lakes dotted about the high ground. To the south your eye follows the lines of the steep escarpment and ranges across the wide green strath about Portmadoc, to rest finally upon the blue waters of Tremadoc Bay. To the west Moel Hebog is a conspicuous feature of the extensive landscape, and beyond its left shoulder you will perceive the shapely lines of the Rivals on a clear day. It is the north-western prospect, however, that will hold your gaze, because from this viewpoint there is an unsurpassed vista of the Snowdon group and the Horseshoe in its entirety. On the left the great ridge rises in one long unbroken sweep to terminate at Y Wyddfa. It undulates over Crib y Ddisgl and then falls to Crib Goch, where the Pinnacles are clearly perceived on its left. Lliwedd does not look so imposing from here, but its three peaks may be discerned in a line with Crib y Ddisgl.

It is a pleasant walk down the long ridge of Cnicht. The grass and heather below is interspersed with stooks of rock. You pass the Dog Lakes, set amid the barren undulations near Ysgafell Wen, and on the right you look down upon the vast marshy valley which is the source of the Afon Lledr. To the north you will see the glittering waters of Llyn Edno, dominated by Moel Siabod. It is one of the larger lakes of the group and a favourite spot for anglers. There are no well-marked tracks here, but you may descend by the banks of the stream which emerges from Llyn Edno and follow its attractive course through many a wild ravine down to the Nantmor Road.

MOEL SIABOD FROM LLYN DINAS

CNICHT FROM THE SOUTH

THE SNOWDON HORSESHOE AND LLYN YR ADAR FROM CNICHT

THE GLYDERS

THE Glyders is the name given to the long ridge stretching in a north-westerly direction from Capel Curig. It comprises a number of well-defined tops of which the most westward is Elidir Fawr, a shapely peak rising above Llyn Peris on the south. The whole group is characterised on the north by a series of wild cwms, whereas on the south the slopes are steep but bereft of striking rock formations with the exception of Esgair Felen, whose shattered cliffs overhang the narrow Llanberis Pass. A few lonely lakes are enclosed in the folds of these hills, but it is the ridge itself which provides the main attraction for the mountaineer, who in the course of a walk along its crest encounters some of the strangest and most fascinating rock architecture in the whole of Snowdonia.

The Glyders may be ascended by a variety of routes, depending on where you stay. Ogwen Cottage is perhaps the best centre owing to its position in relation to the grandest section of the ridge, but the traverse may be undertaken from Pen-y-Pass, provided you do not object to the less interesting ascent and descent. I have walked over the Glyders from various points, including the direct ascent from Capel, and while I am prepared to admit that the most attractive route from the viewpoint of the scrambler is by way of the north ridge of Tryfan, over Bristley Ridge and the two Glyders and then down by the Devil's Kitchen, I consider this circuit is improved upon by the direct ascent from Helyg, because it reveals the east face of Tryfan from a number of viewpoints which are unsurpassed elsewhere. The weird architecture of the ridge is impressive at any time of the year, and although I have seen it during the four seasons, I think it looks its best in winter under really good snow conditions.

You leave Helyg and ascend the ridge enclosing Cwm Tryfan on the east. On your right the majestic buttresses of Tryfan tower above you. The ridge slopes gently upwards and its ascent is easy. When you approach the col giving access to Pen-y-Gwryd, the prospect of Glyder Fach and Bristley Ridge on your right is of Alpine magnificence, with the Pinnacles of the latter adding a grim touch to the scene. The miners' track from Pen-y-Gwryd and Pen-y-Pass reaches the col in the vicinity of this viewpoint, and climbers ascending it will doubtless look back on the view to the south, where the drama of the immense panorama increases with every step. From this belvedere the inn far below seems like a toy building in the vast landscape, and both Lockwood's Llyn and Llyn Gwynant glitter in the sunlight, with the sea glimmering away into the illimitable distance beyond. The great ridge of Gallt y Wenallt makes a superb picture and rises on the right to terminate in the shadowy cliffs of Lliwedd.

The last section of Glyder Fach is steep and full of pitfalls, because in deep snow the spaces between the large boulders are hidden and you have to go carefully. On reaching the summit plateau you see the Cantilever on the left and a little further on gaze in wonder upon the gigantic boulders of Glyder Fach, which resemble some weird arctic picture rather than the summit of the mountain as you know it in summer. To the west Castell y Gwynt stands on the narrow part of the ridge, and in these conditions presents a formidable obstacle. It is better to go over it rather than round its south side, because the deep snow again hides the cavities between the boulders. This strangely beautiful spired castle is the most fascinating of all the Glyders' architecture; if you imagined the structure as resembling crystallised music no one would dispute your analogy.

The panorama in every direction is magnificent on a winter day, and especially so to the south, where Snowdon and his satellites rise into the opalescent sky like the peaks of a celestial fairyland. To the west the ridge slopes up to Glyder Fawr, which is characterised by innumerable outcrops of rock, and you will hasten down to the col, pass the top of the Gribin Ridge on your right, and skirt the fearsome precipices of the Nameless Cwm as you advance towards it. You will linger on this amazing summit to admire the effects of sun, wind, rain and snow on the fantastic groups of rock spread around, and then you will plunge down the steep slippery slopes to the Devil's Kitchen far below.

To look through the narrow icicled walls of Twll Du in winter is an eerie experience, for you catch a glimpse of Llyn Idwal and Llyn Ogwen in the distance while the great snowfields of the Carnedds form a glittering background to the scene. If you walk to the right for a short distance, you will strike the shelf which slopes down to the foot of this fearsome chasm. The descent is slippery and the section below to Llyn Idwal requires care owing to the hidden boulders and snow-filled recesses. The walk thereafter to Ogwen Cottage presents no difficulties, and when you sit by the fire in the evening you may congratulate yourself on having witnessed some of the finest snow scenes in the country.

GALLT Y WENALLT FROM THE GLYDERS

GLYDER FACH AND

BRISTLEY RIDGE

GLYDER FACH

GLYDER FAWR FROM CASTELL Y GWYNT

THE MOEL HEBOG GROUP

MOEL HEBOG is the crowning peak in the range of hills forming the western boundaries of Snowdonia. It rises behind Beddgelert and completely dominates the adjacent landscape, but is seen to better advantage from the Vale of Gwynant some two miles outside the village. The group as a whole is characterised by rounded hills, but its northern outposts are more craggy; indeed, the enclosing walls of the Nantlle Valley raise it to a position of importance in the scenery of Wild Wales.

Moel Hebog itself is easily accessible from Beddgelert, but the northern outliers of the group are remote. While a bicycle is useful for getting to the base of any of these distant climbs, it is of little value when a traverse of the ridge enclosing the south side of the Nantlle Valley is contemplated, because it is necessary to scale the hills in the vicinity of Cwm Silin and walk eastwards along the crest to descend from Y Garn.

The ascent of Moel Hebog is a pleasant walk which may easily be accomplished in a short day. The mountain may be climbed direct from the back of the Goat Hotel, but it is better to make a circular walk of it and go up from the camping site about a mile from the village on the Carnarvon road. The craggy northern ridge enclosing the cwm below the summit should be tackled direct, and although there is no well-marked track, a route will be found without much difficulty. The ridge leads round the face of the mountain, but the actual summit is a long way to the south of it. Moreover, it offers no advantages as a viewpoint: in fact the best belvedere is near the first cairn encountered on the summit plateau. This affords an excellent vista to the north-east, where the houses of Beddgelert are perceived far below and the eye passes over them and along the Vale of Gwynant, to rest finally upon the summit of Moel Siabod. The whole of this range of hills is visible on the right, while the Snowdon peaks assume peculiar shapes high up on the left, and in my opinion, are least impressive when seen from this viewpoint. The descent is at first very rough, but the scree and crags soon give place to grass all the way down to the trees behind the village.

The best walk in the Moel Hebog Group is the traverse of the Nantlle Ridge already alluded to, and if one's lodgings are in Rhyd-ddu, it is possible to walk along the valley as far as Llyn Nantlle Uchaf and then go up to Cwm Silin from the farm beyond the lake. There is a formidable wall enclosing the higher boundaries of the farmstead, and it is difficult to cross it excepting well to the west, where two white stones on its top mark the easiest place. As you scale a large grassy mound ahead, the twin lakes are revealed at the foot of the savage crags encircling the cwm. The conspicuous feature of this impressive array of rock is the Great Slab high up on the left: a severe ascent for the few rock climbers who have tackled it in these remote regions. It is a good scramble up the wild gully on the right of the slab, but some may prefer to go round the cwm, which may easily be accomplished from the crags on the right.

Once you are on the top, follow the ridge eastwards all the way to Y Garn II. It is narrow in places and undulates considerably at its western end, but the views in all directions are magnificent. There are two cairns on the narrow summit of Y Garn and they afford wonderful prospects of Snowdon, whose pendent ridges fall on either side and enclose Cwm Clogwyn with its small lakes, but these are hidden by the ridge of Llechog which sweeps round to the north-west. The view to the north across the depths of the Nantlle Valley is impressive, because the spectacular rotten rock ridges of Craig y Bere are well seen from this belvedere. The descent to the road from Y Garn is precipitous and quite impossible directly below the cairn, but a little way back along the ridge a track leads down a craggy escarpment and then grassy slopes fall to the top of the pass.

MOEL SIABOD, THE GWYNANT VALLEY AND BEDDGELERT FROM MOEL HEBOG

MOEL HEBOG FROM THE AFON GLASLYN

SNOWDON FROM Y GARN II

PEN-Y-PASS AND LLYN LLYDAW

THE Gorphwysfa Hotel stands on the crest of the Llanberis Pass at well over 1,000 feet above the sea. The situation is unique, for the great bastions of Snowdon rise from its very doors and some of the finest climbing grounds are within easy reach, while its altitude means a considerable saving in energy when the Horseshoe is traversed by those who stay there.

It is true enough that Pen-y-Pass is subjected to the buffetings of the westerly gales which sweep through the narrow confines of the pass far below and shriek in wild anger as they tear through the funnel at the col, but the inn was constructed to withstand such onslaughts and the occupants are scarcely conscious of these conditions when they exist. There are other compensations, too, for at sundown on a favourable day, when the mystic purple lights come and go amid the savage cliffs of the superb foreground, the vista to the west is one of gorgeous colouring.

The Inn may be reached from both Llanberis and Bettws-y-Coed, and from either station it is a pleasant walk through attractive country all the way. When you enter its doors, there are signs everywhere of its popularity with the mountaineer; well-oiled boots lie here, coils of rope there, and rucksacks in every corner, while the pictures on the walls portray many of the scenes of mountain grandeur in the vicinity. The cosy sitting-room on the right has a piano, and even during the summer evenings a fire burns in the grate to take off the chilliness of the atmosphere at this altitude. The dining-room on the left is the envy of all the ladies who enter, for the array of gleaming silver suggests assiduous daily polishing, whereas the sulphur-free air is the real secret of its immaculate appearance. You will be happy here, for you may talk mountaineering at any time and have plenty of sympathetic listeners who know and love the places you discourse upon, while there are also reminders of the world-famous climbers who have served their apprenticeship on the surrounding hills.

There are several walks in the vicinity of Pen-y-Pass for the less energetic. One of the best of these is to Cwm Glas, which is hidden from the hotel by the great northern ridge falling from Crib Goch to Dinas Mot. The track contours round its flanks high above the precipices at its base, and enters the cwm at about the 2,000 feet contour. The scene is magnificent, with the small lake of Llyn Glas lying amid wild surroundings and dominated by Crib Goch, whose crest and pinnacles rise to the south. The Parson's Nose falls to the right of this ridge and is one of the popular climbing grounds hereabouts.

Another easy stroll is to Llyn Llydaw by way of the cart track opposite the inn. You walk along its rough surface with fine prospects of the Moel Siabod group to the east, and when it bends to the right to Cwm Dyli the great sweep of the Snowdon Horseshoe is revealed. The steep slabs of Lliwedd first come into view on the left, and as you round the bend the conical summit of Snowdon appears over the low shoulder of the hill and you afterwards perceive the eastern *arête* of Crib Goch high up on the right, but the mountain looks less shapely from here than from Pen-y-Pass. The ridge connecting these two peaks over Crib y Ddisgl is, however, not seen to advantage and appears somewhat foreshortened. The cart track passes Llyn Teyrn low down on the left and then crosses the flanks of the hill to emerge finally on the shore of Llyn Llydaw at the foot of Snowdon. The scene is one of wild grandeur and is at all times impressive, but when the vast amphitheatre of the cwm is clad in snow, its cliffs look magnificent in the early morning sun.

There are times when the splendour of Cwm Dyli is transformed by storms into a wild workshop of the Titans. On one occasion I was there when low clouds curtained the high peaks and were driven eastwards by a stiff breeze from the Atlantic. The engirdling cliffs were grim and forbidding, in strange contrast with the sunlit hills some miles to the east. The dark waters of the lake were churned into foam as they beat upon the shore, while black clouds rolled over the Pass of the Arrows and wreaths of mist swept along the flanks of Lliwedd and Crib Goch. Suddenly a shaft of low sunlight appeared over Bwlch-y-Saethau and cast its rays upon the turbulent waters of Llyn Llydaw, touching everything in its path with a dull burnish of gold. It was only a transient glimpse of one of nature's metamorphoses in which the mystic lighting revealed this wild cwm in a strangely fascinating mood.

From Llyn Llydaw it is a good walk along the climbers' track to the foot of the Lliwedd precipices, but this path is followed only by mountaineers. The pedestrian, however, may cross the Causeway and climb the Miners' Track to Glaslyn, hidden in a rocky basin at the foot of the precipices of Y Wyddfa. The path rises ahead and, as the Zig-Zags, reaches the col which gives easy access to the summit of the reigning peak.

THE GLYDERS FROM PEN-Y-PASS

SNOWDON AND CRIB GOCH

SNOWDON FROM LLYN LLYDAW

THE SNOWDON HORSESHOE

THE Snowdon Horseshoe provides one the finest mountain 'walks' in the whole of Britain, and a description of its traverse seems a fitting conclusion to this book. The ridge constitutes the engirdling crest of the vast amphitheatre of Cwm Dyli and includes four well-defined peaks, Crib Goch, Crib y Ddisgl, Y Wyddfa and Lliwedd. The circuit covers a map distance of about seven and a half miles, and since it usually begins and ends at Pen-y-Pass, it involves some 6,000 feet of climbing.

Crib Goch is the north-eastern sentinel of the Horseshoe. Its fine pyramid rises into the western sky from the very doors of the Gorphwysfa Hotel and beckons irresistibly to all climbers who stay there. A well-worn track rises to Bwlch Moch and it is a good pull to this col, which affords excellent views across Cwm Dyli, where the great slabs of Lliwedd rise precipitously above the scree enclosing the dark waters of Llyn Llydaw far below. The main path, known as the Pyg Track, skirts the southern flanks of Crib Goch and joins the Miners' Track well above Glaslyn. The Horseshoe follows the crest of the ridge and grass soon gives place to steep reddish crags which, as a great rock staircase, constitutes the eastern *arête* of Crib Goch.

This part of the ascent is most enjoyable, and with every step the immensity of the vast landscape increases. The summit sails high above in the sky, while low down on the right, there is a glimpse of the thin line of the Llanberis Pass. The *arête* becomes very narrow and sensational, and finally ends at the small cairn where there is just enough room for a few people to sit together. From this unrivalled belvedere the eye is greeted in every direction by scenes of savage grandeur.

Imagine that you are standing on this isolated summit of Crib Goch, where the precipitous cliffs fall away at such a steep angle to the north, south and east that you are unable to follow their contours down for more than 50 or 60 feet. You feel poised in the sky, surrounded by vast space, while to the west a narrow knife-edge joins your viewpoint to the terrestrial sphere. The only sound intruding upon the strange silence is the eerie wind sobbing in the gullies below, while above you the clouds now appear so near that you can almost grasp them.

Looking westwards you follow the undulating line of the narrow crest on which you are standing towards the pinnacles that seem to end your possible avenue of escape. Beneath them on the right you observe a grassy continuation of the ridge which, as it rises again, becomes more craggy until it culminates in the summit of Carnedd Ugain; then sweeping round gracefully to the left, it ends on the cone of Y Wyddfa.

Your gaze rests on this beautiful peak of Snowdon, which from your lofty perch displays such lovely lines, with its eastern precipices falling to the blue-green waters of Glaslyn. Below you on the right you look down into the vast abysmal depths of Cwm Glas, where the small crag-encircled lake glitters like an emerald at the foot of the Parson's Nose. On looking back you perceive the white walls of Pen-y-Pass far below, now a spot in the vast landscape which stretches away to the east where the Capel lakes catch the light on the left of Moel Siabod.

You will linger here entranced by this scene of superlative splendour, but there is still much ground to cover, so you scramble carefully over the sensational knife-edge ridge and cross the giddy pinnacles to join the path below, which leads to Carnedd Ugain. The Horseshoe sweeps round to the left and it is only a short step past the cairn standing at the top of the Zig-Zags to the summit of the reigning peak.

The panorama from Y Wyddfa embraces immense scenes which are limited only by the clarity of the atmosphere, and on a clear day are said to reveal peaks as far distant as Scafell in English Lakeland. It is, however, the ridges falling away below you that will attract your attention. To the north Crib y Ddisgl sweeps down to Crib Goch and is backed by the vast solitudes of the Glyders, with beyond them, a glimpse of Carnedd Llewelyn. To the south your eye follows the thin line of the Watkin Path and after following the ridge forming the second half of the Horseshoe, rests finally upon the savage cliffs of Lliwedd suspended above the empty solitudes of Cwm Dyli far below.

You descend the loose slippery slopes of Snowdon in this direction and walk along the enclosing walls of the cwm, past Bwlch-y-Saethau, and scramble up the narrow rock *arête* leading to Lliwedd. On your left you look down on the dark waters of Llyn Llydaw, and when you reach the first summit, gaze in admiration upon the terrific precipices of the East Peak of Lliwedd; a rock climber's paradise and one of the most popular in all Snowdonia.

The track keeps to the crest of the precipices all the way over Lliwedd Bach and finally descends to the shore of the lake by steep grass slopes, the cart track ultimately leading back to Pen-y-Pass.

CRIB GOCH FROM PEN-Y-PASS

THE FIRST HALF OF THE SNOWDON HORSESHO

SNOWDON AND CRIB Y DDISGL FROM CRIB GOCH

CRIB GOCH FROM THE SUMMIT OF SNOWDON

THE SECOND HALF OF THE HORSESHOE—LLIWEDD FROM SNOWDON

THE GLYDERS AND LLYN LLYDAW FROM LLIWEDD

THE EAST PEAK OF LLIWEDD

LOOKING BACK TO LLIWEDD FROM LLYN LLYDAW

INDEX